P9-DXH-584

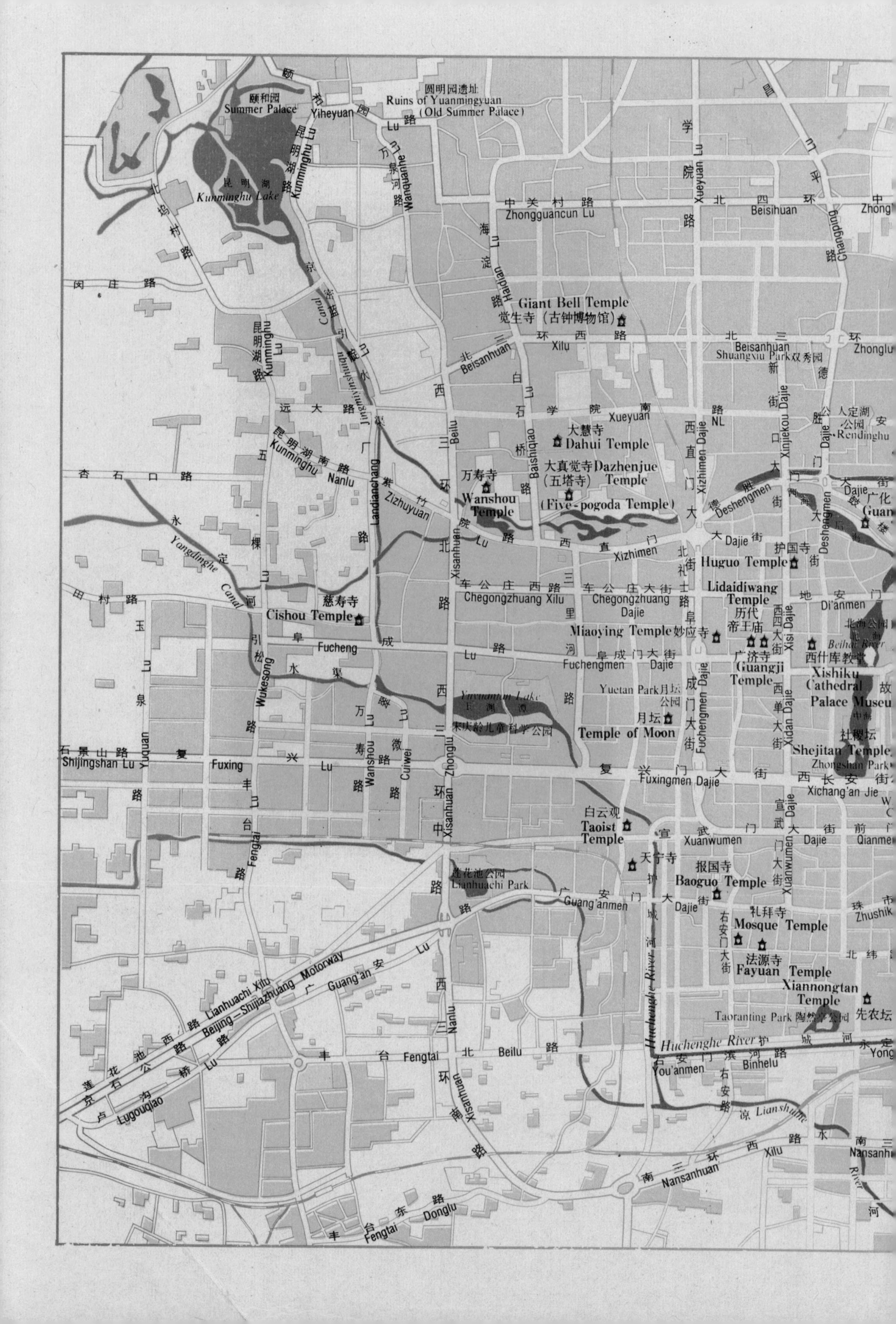

颐和园
Summary Palace
圆明园遗址
Ruins of Yuanmingyuan
(Old Summer Palace)
Yiheyuan
Lu
昆明湖
Kunminghu Lake
Kunminghu Lu
Wanquanhe
中关村路
Zhongguancun Lu
Xueyuan Lu
Beisihuan
Haidian Lu
Giant Bell Temple
觉生寺（古钟博物馆）
Xilu
Beisanhuan
Shuangxiu Park 双秀园
Zhonglu
Canal
Jingmiyinshui
Kunminghu
Xueyuan
大慧寺
Dahui Temple
大真觉寺 Dazhenjue
(五塔寺) Temple
(Five-pogoda Temple)
万寿寺
Wanshou Temple
Baishiqiao
Beilu
Kunminghu Nanlu
Zizhuyuan
Landianchang
Xizhimen Dajie
Xinjiekou Dajie
Deshengmen
Xizhimen
Yangdinghe
Canal
Huguo Temple
护国寺
Lidaidiwang Temple
历代帝王庙
Di'anmen
Chegongzhuang Xilu
Chegongzhuang Dajie
慈寿寺
Cishou Temple
Miaoying Temple 妙应寺
广济寺
Guangji Temple
西什库教堂
Xishiku Cathedral
Palace Museu
Fucheng
Lu
Fuchengmen Dajie
Yuetan Park 月坛公园
月坛
Temple of Moon
Fuchengmen Dajie
Xidan Dajie
Xisi Dajie
Yuyuantan Lake
宋庆龄儿童科学公园
社稷坛
Shejitan Temple
Zhongshan Park
Wukesong
Yuquan
Shijingshan Lu
Fuxing
Lu
Wanshou
Cuiwei
Zhonglu
Fuxingmen Dajie
Xichang'an Jie
白云观
Taoist Temple
Xisanhuan
Fengtai
Xuanwumen
Dajie
Qianme
天宁寺
报国寺
Baoguo Temple
Xuanwumen Dajie
莲花池公园
Lianhuachi Park
Guang'anmen
Dajie
礼拜寺
Mosque Temple
Zhushik
法源寺
Fayuan Temple
Xiannongtan Temple
先农坛
Taoranting Park 陶然亭公园
Lianhuachi Xilu
Beijing-Shijiazhuang Motorway
Guang'an Lu
Lu
Hucheng River
Huchenghe River
Fengtai
Beilu
Binhelu
You'anmen
Yong
Lugouqiao
Xisanhuan Nanlu
Lianshuihe
Xilu
Nansanhuan
Nansanh
River
Fengtai Donglu

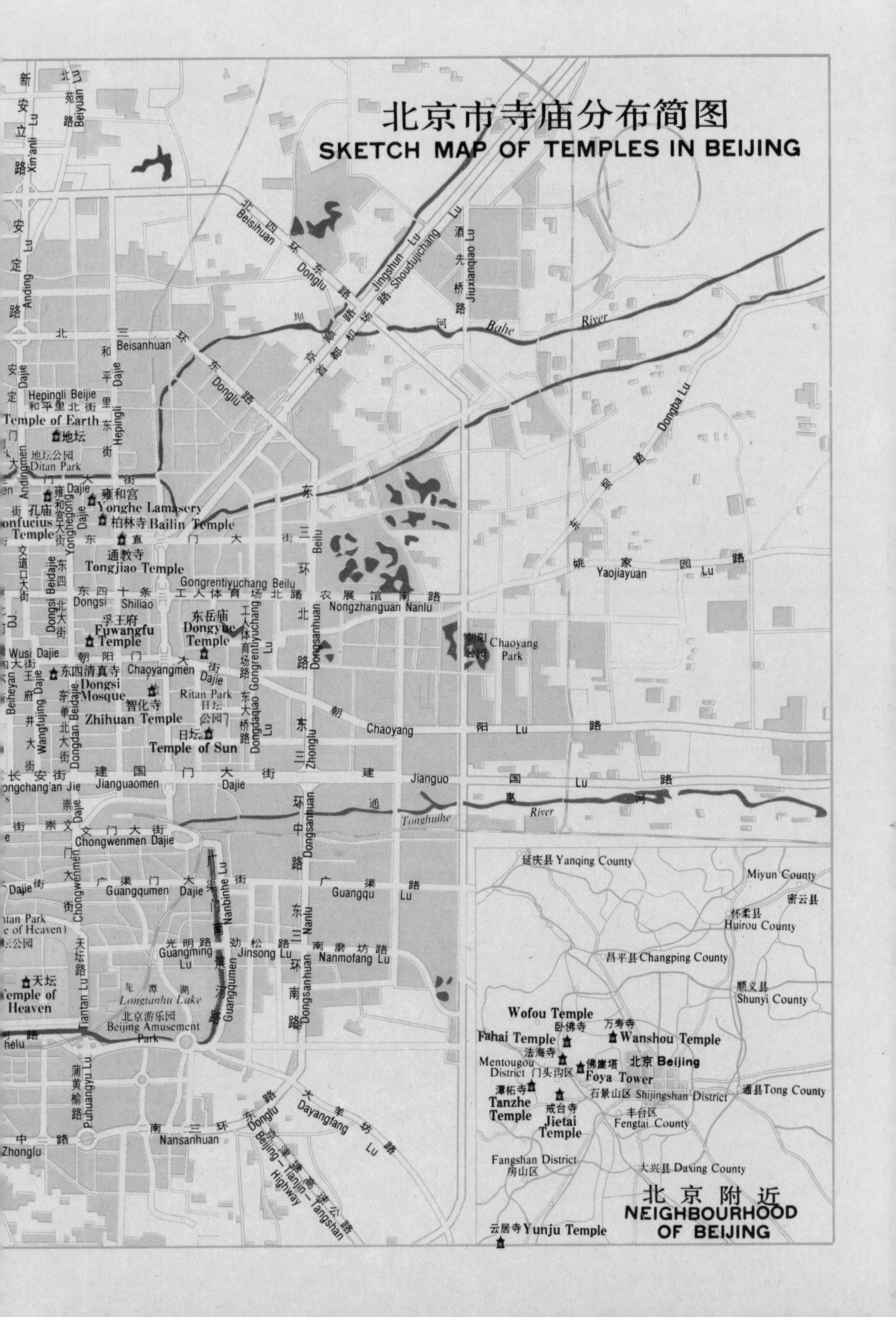

北京市寺庙分布简图
SKETCH MAP OF TEMPLES IN BEIJING
Temple of Earth
地坛
地坛公园
Ditan Park
雍和宫
Yonghe Lamasery
孔庙
Confucius Temple
柏林寺 Bailin Temple
通教寺
Tongjiao Temple
孚王府
Fuwangfu Temple
东岳庙
Dongyue Temple
东四清真寺
Dongsi Mosque
智化寺
Zhihuan Temple
日坛公园
Ritan Park
日坛
Temple of Sun
天坛
Temple of Heaven
龙潭湖
Longtanhu Lake
北京游乐园
Beijing Amusement Park
朝阳公园
Chaoyang Park
Beisihuan Donglu
Jingshun Lu
Shoudujichang Lu
Jiuxianqiao Lu
Bahe River
Beisanhuan
Donglu
Dongba Lu
Yaojiayuan Lu
Gongrentiyuchang Beilu
Nongzhanguan Nanlu
Dongsanhuan Beilu
Chaoyangmen Dajie
Chaoyang Lu
Jianguomen Dajie
Jianguo Lu
Tonghuihe River
Chongwenmen Dajie
Guangqumen Dajie
Guangqu Lu
Guangming Lu
Jinsong Lu
Nanmofang Lu
Nansanhuan
Dayangfang Lu
Beijing—Tianjin—Tangshan Highway
Xin'anli Lu
Beiyuan Lu
Anding Lu
Hepingli Beijie
Hepingli Dajie
Andingmen Dajie
Yonghegong Dajie
Dongsi Beidajie
Dongsi Shiliao
Wusi Dajie
Wangfujing Dajie
Dongdan Beidajie
Chang'an Jie
Chongwenmen
Tiantan Lu
Puhuangyu Lu
Zhonglu
延庆县 Yanqing County
Miyun County
密云县
怀柔县
Huirou County
昌平县 Changping County
顺义县
Shunyi County
Wofou Temple
卧佛寺
万寿寺
Wanshou Temple
Fahai Temple
法海寺
Mentougou District 门头沟区
佛崖塔
Foya Tower
北京 Beijing
通县 Tong County
潭柘寺
Tanzhe Temple
戒台寺
Jietai Temple
石景山区 Shijingshan District
丰台区
Fengtai County
Fangshan District
房山区
大兴县 Daxing County
北京附近
NEIGHBOURHOOD OF BEIJING
云居寺 Yunju Temple

十一面千手千眼观音
（清）

北京古刹名寺

樸初題

ANCIENT TEMPLES IN BEIJING

中国世界语出版社
PUBLISHED BY CHINA ESPERANTO PRESS, BEIJING

Second edition 1995

ISBN 7-5052-0118-2

Published by the China Esperanto Press, P. O. Box 77. Beijing, China

Distributed by China International Book Trading Corporation (Guoji Shudian)
35 W. Chegongzhuang Xilu, Beijing, China
P. O. Box 399, Post code: 100044

目　录
CONTENTS

北京寺庙古今谈

“先有潭柘，后有幽州”

北京西郊潭柘山中，深藏着一座佛寺，它背倚翠峰，面对平野，东、西、北三面环列着九座峰峦，古人形象地称之为“九龙戏珠”、“碧莲花里梵王宫”。这座选址绝妙的寺院就是建于晋代（公元 265–420 年）的潭柘寺（初建时名嘉福寺），它是北京地区最早出现的寺庙。一句久为流传的民谚说“先有潭柘，后有幽州”，正道出了这座寺庙建造年代的悠远。

北京地区出现城邑约在公元前十一世纪，当时名蓟，是一方国都城。潭柘寺创建时，蓟城是统一的西晋王朝（公元 265–316 年）的辖地幽州的治所、北方的军事重镇。公元七世纪初，唐王朝（公元 618–907 年）兴建，新王朝为图兴求治，大力整修、加固蓟城城垣，在城内划分街坊，营造官署。此时蓟城虽然仍为幽州治所，但是，幽州城却成了它的别称，其位置在今北京市区西南部，有的街道方位至今未变。

潭柘寺创建之时，正值佛教在蓟地开始流行，这时距佛教传入中国和中国第一座佛寺的建立已经两个多世纪了。

佛教于公元前六至五世纪时创立于印度，并在本土得以传播、发展，至公元前三世纪开始向境外传播。公元前一世纪佛教随着骆驼商队经由古丝绸之路从印度传至中亚细亚和中国的新疆，而后进入中国内地。传说佛教在中国流传得力于汉明帝刘庄（公元 58–75 年在位），他受了梦的启示，派遣十几名大臣出使天竺，访求佛法，使臣们行至大月氏（今阿富汗、中亚一带）时，遇到天竺高僧摄摩腾、竺法蓝，并得到佛像和佛经，遂邀同二高僧，用白马驮负佛像、佛经，于公元 67 年共返汉都洛阳。

二位高僧抵达洛阳后，刘庄在洛阳东郊仿照天竺佛寺的样式修建了一座僧院，供他们居住。为了纪念背负经像的白马，取名为白马寺。

“寺”本是中国古代官署名称，其建筑之豪华，门禁之森严，地位之尊崇仅次于帝王居住的宫殿。供奉佛像和安置天竺高僧的处所被视为与官署等同的神圣之地，所以命名为“寺”，这便是中国有佛寺之始。

隋窟唐寺

西晋王朝的统一局面只维持了半个世纪，于公元 316 年被北方匈奴贵族集团所灭。第二年晋朝皇族司马睿在建康（今江苏南京）称帝，建立了偏安江南的东晋王朝（公元 317–420 年）。从此，中国陷入无休止的战乱之中。北方各族纷争，呈现分裂割据状态；南方朝代更迭频繁，皇族间互相杀戮。当时，下层百姓自是苦不堪言，就连皇家贵族也感到生死无常，荣辱瞬变。佛教宣扬“因果报应”、“生死轮回”，劝导人们安生知命，寄希望于来生，因而召来了众多信徒，广泛流传开来，随之建寺凿窟之风大兴。

西晋之后，蓟城所处的北地，虽然政权

屡易其主，但大多数当政者对于佛教都采取扶持的态度。至北魏（公元 386—534 年）末，北方寺院多达三万余。至今在北京海淀温泉附近，尚留存一尊北魏时雕刻的石佛像。像高 2.2 米，是北京现存最古老的石雕佛像。今广安门外的天宁寺也是北魏时创建的，当时名光林寺。

隋（公元 581—618 年）、唐时期，中国南北归于一统，两朝帝王为利于王朝的统一和巩固，大力扶持、提倡佛教，并加强管理，使佛教发展达到极盛。那时北京地区分别称涿郡和幽州，均为幽州治所。这一时期兴建或重建于此的寺、塔主要有云居寺、弘业寺（即北魏时的光林寺）、悯忠寺（今法源寺），以及道教寺院天长观（今白云观）等。

云居寺位于今北京西南石经山西麓，隋大业年间（公元 605—617 年）僧人静琬（公元？—639 年）在石经山腰开凿石窟，埋藏所刻石板经，后又在山下建寺。静琬此举缘起于隋以前的两次废佛事件。公元 446 年和 574 年，北魏太武帝和北周（公元 557—581 年）武帝诏令僧尼还俗，“废法灭佛”，佛教僧众称之为“法难”。静琬的师父慧思大师经历了北周武帝灭佛之劫以后，决意将经文镌刻在石板上，封藏于岩壑之中保存。而在此以前经文都抄写在绢帛和皮纸上，极易被毁。静琬为了却师父的遗愿，自七世纪初，至公元 639 年逝世，三十余年刻经不止，将所刻的石经“藏诸室内，每一室满，即以石塞门，熔铁锢之”。静琬去世后，他的弟子们相继主持镌刻。此项工程经隋、唐、辽、金、元、明，延续至十七世纪，共刻经一千余部，现存完好的刻石 14278 块，成为国之重宝。

今宣武门外的法源寺初建于唐代，是北京的名刹之一。唐代初期，太宗李世民（公元 627—649 年在位）进兵辽东，并亲自前往督战，结果久战不胜，伤亡惨重，回师途经幽州时，他下令在城中建佛寺悼念阵亡将士，以安抚军心。寺至 696 年建成，赐名悯忠寺。据史籍记载，唐代寺内曾有一座悯忠阁，高耸巍峨，民谚说“悯忠寺阁，去天一握”。由于年代久远，悯忠阁连同初建时的殿宇均已毁圮，当年的旧貌已不可知。但是，从文献记载中，以及国内一些得以幸存的唐寺殿宇，可以得知唐时佛寺的布局、规模，乃至建筑风格，较之佛教初传入时所建的寺院有了很大的变化。

中国早期佛寺的平面布局仿印度式样，塔建于寺的中心，内藏舍利，供信徒礼拜，四周配置僧房、佛殿。建于一世纪中叶的第一座佛寺白马寺采用的就是这种格局。寺的主体为一大型方木塔，居寺中心，四周围以殿廊僧房。后来渐渐融入中国宫殿、官署常采用的以中轴线布署的院落式格局。一般前有寺门，门内建塔，塔后建佛殿，内供佛像。随着时间推移，供奉佛像和僧侣诵经的殿堂升至与塔并重的地位，二者在寺中的方位也由塔在殿前而变为塔殿并列。时至七世纪的唐代，僧人道宣（公元 596—667 年）根据中国传统建筑布局的特点制《戒坛图经》，将佛寺的布局改为以佛殿为中心，塔的位置退至寺旁、寺后，或另建塔院。

唐代以后，中国建筑讲求迂回曲折、步移景换和有林泉之奇、山居之妙的造景艺术。佛寺建筑也受此影响，在保持对称统一格局的同时，另在寺内营建有园林之胜的景点。

印度传入的佛寺就这样被逐步中国化了。

“僧居之寺，冠于北方”

十世纪初，崛起于内蒙古高原的契丹族建立起辽朝，势力扩至华北北部。公元 938

年，幽州城成为辽朝的五座京城之一，称作南京，又名燕京。

辽代的当权者为使人心归附，大力提倡佛教，优礼僧徒，在辖地建寺造塔，汇刻佛经。笃信佛教的王室权贵、豪门富户广施金钱、庄田给寺院。此时燕京城内外庙宇相望，据记载仅城内规模较大的庙宇就有36座。那时城内外供帝王居住游赏的宫殿苑囿尚寥寥无几，这些建得雄伟弘丽的寺庙成了主要名胜。故而《辽志》说燕京的“僧居之寺，冠于北方”。可惜当时的寺庙，今日已无从窥见，仅能透过残留的古塔断碑，追思昔日的繁盛。

位于西郊晹台山间的大觉寺，其前身为辽代创建的清水院，至今该寺仍保留初建时背西面东的方位，这是契丹族朝日习俗的遗痕。

北京建清真寺起于辽代。公元996年，一位从阿拉伯来中国传教的法师之子，在回族聚集的牛街建立一座清真寺，这便是至今尚存的北京规模最大的牛街礼拜寺。

相传辽代时曾在燕京城的五方各建一塔，塔分五色，青、黑等四塔后来毁于兵燹，唯白塔独存，即今日阜成门内妙应寺白塔的前身。建于辽代留存至今的寺塔尚有今广安门外的天宁寺塔、云居寺塔等。

塔是重要的宗教建筑之一，也是从印度随佛教传入中国的，印度的塔有两种，一种是埋藏佛和高僧的舍利、骨齿遗骸的坟冢式塔，称窣堵波。早期的窣堵波为覆钵式大土冢，上有伞盖，底部有台基和围栏，前面设有供上下的阶梯。妙应寺白塔的形制即与此一脉相承。印度的另一种佛塔是建在石窟内的，称为支提，传入中国后发展成立于石窟中央的塔柱。中国的佛塔是由覆钵式窣堵波与中国传统的建筑形式融合、演变而成的。其质料有木、石、砖、金、银、铜、铁、陶、琉璃等，其平面形状分为四方形、圆形和六角、八角、十二角形等，其结构形式有楼阁式、亭阁式、密檐式、覆钵式、金刚宝座式，以及花塔、过街塔等。它们的种类和功能远远超过了印度的佛塔。

继辽之后，女真族所建的金朝（公元1115－1234年）迁都燕京，将其名改为中都。一批供皇室贵族居住游赏的宫室别苑在中都城内应时而建，修建寺塔之风盛于前代，都城之内，佛寺数以百计。著名的有弥陀寺、护圣寺、香山寺、圣安寺、隆恩寺、功德寺、香林禅寺、雀儿庵等。道观有玉虚、天长、崇福、修真等。

帝都名刹

公元1271年，蒙古族首领忽必烈（公元1260－1294年在位）建立了元帝国，并耗时二十年在金中都的东北郊筑建新城，作为国都，称之为大都。又于1279年和1234年分别灭南宋（公元1127－1279年）和金，中国重归一统，从此北京取代了长安（今陕西西安）、洛阳、汴梁（今河南开封）等古都的地位，成为统一的中央王朝的都城，并延至明（公元1368－1644年）、清（公元1644－1911年），时达640年。

元、明、清三代时的北京城内外，宝刹林立，香火旺盛。据记载明代北京共有寺院千余所。清代绘制的《乾隆京城全图》上标有胡同约1400条，而寺庙竟达1300余座，几乎每条胡同里都有寺庙。这一时期，许多寺庙经过多次扩建，成为闻名于世的巨刹。如元代耗巨资扩建唐兜率寺，冶铜25吨，铸成长5米余的卧佛，供于寺殿中，以致寺以佛闻名，被称为卧佛寺。此时寺庙建筑中出现了具有艺术水平很高的雕塑和绘画。今北京石景山区法海寺内的壁画、西直门外大慧寺内的彩塑、五塔寺金刚宝座塔基座上的雕刻、觉生寺内铸造精美的巨钟，都是明代的杰作。清代在碧云寺内建造的金刚宝座塔和五百罗汉，成为该寺最精湛的建筑和雕塑。

元代尊佛崇道，朝廷明令蠲免道院、出家人的赋税，因此，道教徒甚众，道教盛极一时。

道教是产生于中国的宗教，创建于公元二世纪，奉春秋时期（公元前 770－前 476 年）思想家老子为教主，以其著作中有关“道”的内容作为根本信仰和制订教理、教义的依据。道教创立后在历史上曾几度盛行，元代极盛，明代继续流行，至清代渐渐衰微。

元时，藏传佛教（俗称喇嘛教）也得到皇帝的尊崇。

一时间中国境内各种宗教及其各教派同时流行，延续至明、清未变。因此，元、明、清三代，北京地区佛、道、藏传佛教的寺庙和伊斯兰教的清真寺并存，元时大都城内还开始建起了天主教堂。

元大都的道教观院都建得气势不凡。始建于八世纪的天长观，于公元 1227 年奉诏改名长春宫，后又重加修建，历时 20 年方告竣，工程之浩大，由此可见。大都齐化门外的东岳仁圣宫兴建于 1322 年，是道教正一派在华北地区的第一大观。

明代在北京创建或重建了 4 座著名的清真寺，即牛街礼拜寺、东四清真寺、安定门清真寺和锦什坊清真寺。

清代修建的几座喇嘛庙堪称京都名刹。其中最为壮观的首推雍和宫。它原是清世宗雍正（公元 1723－1735 年在位）称帝前的府邸，建筑形制如同帝宫，改建成寺院自然不同一般。安定门外的东、西黄寺和西郊香山的宗镜大昭之庙也建于清代，寺内建筑融合了汉、藏和印度的建筑特色，风格特异。

中国佛教至近代急剧衰落，加之战火连绵和年久失修，北京寺庙有减无增。尽管如此，所存寺庙的数量仍居中国其他城市之首。人们无论漫步于市区，或出游京郊四野，都可见到古塔梵宇的踪迹：或是与现代化楼群并存的寺宇，或是耸立于立交桥畔的古塔，或是掩映在山林中的高阁红墙……

北京及其四郊宛如一座巨大的古寺博物馆，集中了 1500 多年间历朝所建的寺庙。近十几年来，有关部门在一些寺内辟建富有特色的陈列馆，如大钟寺古钟博物馆、正觉寺碑刻陈列馆、云居寺经版陈列馆、万寿寺艺术博物馆，以及正在筹建的报国寺商业博物馆，等等。它们成了北京这座古寺博物馆中的“馆中之馆”。

现存的北京寺庙同故宫、长城、十三陵等文化遗存一样，是中华民族璀璨文化遗产的一部分，它们的价值和功能早已超越了建造者们的本意。如今，这些寺庙虽然依旧是信仰者们从事宗教活动的场所，但是研究者们亦可从这里寻找到建筑、雕塑、绘画、文学和民风世俗等方面的实物资料；游赏者从这里得到美的享受，在浓重的宗教氛围中回顾、辨析历史。而那千百年历久不衰的庙会和异趣纷陈的宗教节日，又为北京市民的经济生活和文化生活增添了新的内容。

ANCIENT TEMPLES IN BEIJING

"TANZHE TEMPLE CAME BEFORE YOUZHOU CITY"

The Buddhist Tanzhe Temple in the Tanzhe Mountains in the western suburbs of Beijing is surrounded by nine peaks on the east, west and north and faces flat land on the south. In old times people discribed the temple as a "pearl played by nine dragons." It was built during the Jin Dynasty (A.D. 265-420), making it the oldest temple in the Beijing area. People often say that "Tanzhe Temple came before Youzhou."

The city of Ji, the capital of a small kingdom, was built in about the 11th century B.C. By the Jin Dynasty it became a strategic point under the jurisdiction of Youzhou Prefecture. In the beginning of the 7th century, the court of the Tang Dynasty (A.D. 618-907) reinforced the city wall, planned the layout of streets there and built government offices within the city of Ji. As its importance rose Ji became commonly known as Youzhou. Its location is in the southwestern part of today's urban area of Beijing. The layout of some of the streets has remained the same.

Tanzhe Temple was built at a time when Buddhism had begun to spread in the Youzhou area, 200 years since Buddhism was introduced into and the first Buddhist temple was built in China.

Buddhism was founded in India between the 6th and 5th centuries B.C. In the 3rd century B.C. it began to spread to other countries. The religion was brought to China by merchants on the Old Silk Road to Central Asia, Xinjiang and further to the hinterland of China in the first century. Some history books attribute the propagation of Buddhism in China to Emperor Mingdi (Liu Zhuang, reigned between A.D. 58-75). Inspired by a dream he sent a dozen court officials to fetch Buddhist scriptures from India. When the envoys came to Darouzhi (present-day Afghanistan and Central Asia), they met two Indian monks, Kasyapa-matanga and Dharmaranya. They invited the two monks to come to Luoyang, capital of the Tang Dynasty, in A.D. 68.

Emperor Mingdi built a temple of Indian style in the eastern suburbs of Louyang as the two monks' residence and to house the Buddha portraits and scriptures they had brought with them. The temple was named White Horse in honor of the white horse which had carried the Buddha portraits and scriptures.

In Chinese the character for temple is "si", which means a grand mansion for high ranking officials, only less magnificent than the imperial palace. Emperor Mingdi named the residence for the two monks si to show how highly he respected Buddhism.

SUI GROTTOES AND TANG TEMPLES

The Western Jin Dynasty lasted only for 50 years. It was overthrown by the Huns from the north in A.D. 316. The next year, Sima Jun, a member of the Jin royal clan, set up the Eastern Jin Dynasty (A.D. 317-420) in Jiankang (present-day Nanjing in Jiangsu Province). China was plunged into chaos. In the north rival tribes fought constant wars; in the south one government replaced another quickly; members of the royal clan killed each other for power; common people led a miserable life and nobilities worried about the safety of their lives. Buddhism advocates "retribution"and "samsara", urging people to depend on fate and place hope on the next life. Frustrated in reality, many people went to Buddhism for consolation. Thus Buddhism spread quickly.

The north where Youzhou was located saw the change of power frequently. But most of the rulers supported Buddhism. By the time of the Northern Wei Dynasty (A.D.386-534) the number of Buddhist temples in the north had reached 30,000. A 2.2-meter-high stone Buddha statue carved during that time near Wenquan in Haidian District is the oldest Buddha statue in existence in Beijing. Tianning Temple outside the city gate of Guang'anmen was built during the Northern Wei Dynasty, called Guanglin Temple then.

North China was unified during the Sui Dynasty (A.D.581-618) and Tang Dynasty. The rulers of the two dynasties all promoted Buddhism as a means to consolidate their power. Buddhism saw its heyday during this period. The Beijing area was divided into Zhuojun and Youzhou, both under the jurisdiction of Youzhou Prefecture. Main temples and pagodas built during this period include Yunju Temple, Hongyue Temple (called Guanglin Temple during the Northern Wei Dynasty), Minzhong Temple (today's Fayou Temple), and the Taoist Tianchang Monastery.

The Yunju Temple is located on the Shijing Mountains southwest of Beijing proper. During the period of Dayue (A.D.605-517) Buddhist monk Jingwan (?-639) began to dig caves in the stone mountainside to hide stone slabs inscribed with scriptures. He did so as a result of two suppressons which took place respectively in A.D.446 and A.D.574. Northern Wei Emperor Wudi and Northern Zhou Emperor Wudi ordered Buddhist monks and nuns to resume secular life. Buddhist followers called the two incidents as "disasters of the law". Monk Hui'en, teacher of Monk Jingwan, decided to carve scriptures on stone slabs and hide them in mountain caves. In earlier days the scriptures were written on silk or leather. Monk Hui'en died. Monk Jingwan carried on the project over 30 years until his death in A.D.639. When he filled up a cave with stone slabs inscribed with scriptures he would block the cave mouth with stone and seal it with melted iron. His disciples continued the carving into the 17th century. More than 1,000 volumes of scriptures were carved on stone slabs. Now the 14,278 stone slabs that have been well preserved are national treasures.

The Fayou Temple outside the city gate of Xuanwumen is one of famous temples in Beijing. It was built in the beginning of the Tang Dynasty. Tang Emperor Taizong (Li Shimin, reigned between A.D.627 and 649) led expedition troops to Liaodong. It turned out to be a protracted war. He suffered a lot of losses and was forced to withdraw. When he arrived in Youzhou he had a temple built and named it Minzhong in memory of dead soldiers. The temple was completed in A.D. 696. History books record there was a high tower in the temple, so high that people said "it could reach the sky within a distance of a fist." The tower and halls had been destroyed long ago. Temples built during the Tang Dynasty that have remained in other places show that the layout, size and architectural style had changed a great deal since Buddhism was first introduced into China.

• The earliest temples followed the style of those of India. There was a pagoda at the center of a temple to house relics. Monks bedrooms and the prayer hall were arranged on four sides around the pagoda. The White Horse Temple, China's first Buddhist temple built in the middle of the first century is of this layout: a wooden pagoda in the center and halls and houses around it. Later temples were much like Chinese palaces or government offices with main buildings arranged along a central axis. Usually within the front gate was a pagoda and behind which the main hall where Buddha portraits and statues were worshipped. As time went on the prayer hall became as important as the pagoda and thus was arranged to be next to it. In the 7th century Monk Dao Xuan (A.D.596-667) changed the layout to make the prayer hall as the center. The pagoda was located either on the side, in the back yard, or in a separate place.

After the Tang Dynasty, Chinese architecture stressed changing scenes with meandering paths, trees, foundains and hills. Influenced by the trend, Buddhist temples also had gardens within them. Thus the architecture of temples became total Chinese.

THE NORTH HAD THE LARGEST NUMBER OF TEMPLES

In the beginning of the 10th century, the Qidan tribes in Inner Mongolia founded the Liao Dynasty. Their influence gradually reached to the northern part of North China. In A.D.938 Youzhou was made one of the five capitals of the Liao Dynasty and was named Nanjing, also known as Yanjing.

To win the support of the people, the Liao rulers made great effort to promote Buddhism. They built temples and pagodas and distributed scriptures. Members of the royal clan and aristocrats donated money and land to temples. History books record 36 large temples within the city. At that time the city hadfew imperial palaces and gardens. Those magnificent temples looked very attractive. The History of the Liao Dynasty writes: Yanjing "had the largest number of temples in the north." But today only some pagodas and broken stone tablets have left from those days.

The Dajue Temple in the Yangtai Mountains in the western suburbs of Beijing was built on the site of Qingshuiyuan Temple of the Liao Dynasty. It faces east, a custom of the Qidan tribes who worshipped the rising sun.

The first mosque appeared in Beijing during the Liao Dynasty. In A.D. 996 the son of a rabbi from Arab came to China to spread Islam and built a mosque on Niujie Street where Moslems lived in a compact community. The mosque has survived and become the largest mosque in Beijing.

During the Liao Dynasty there were five pagodas of five colors in five directions. Four pagodas were destroyed in war. Only the white pagoda has remained intact, which stands inside the Miaoying Temple inside the city gate of Fuchengmen. Pagodas that have remained from the Liao Dynasty today are those in theTianning Temple outside the city gate of Guang'anmen and in the Yunjun Temple.. Pagoda is a major part of the temple. There are two kinds of pagodas in India. One kind is called stupa for keeping the relics and remains of dead high monks. It is built like an overturned bowl with a canopy, raised base and balustrade. A flight of steps in front is used to walk up and down the stupa. The White Pagoda in the Miaoying Temple is of this kind. The other kind is built inside grottoes. In China this kind was eventually turned into the central pillar in a stone cave. Buddhist pagodas in China evolved from Indian stupas with strong Chinese traditional architectural features. They are built of wood, stone, bricks, gold, silver, copper, iron, porcelain or glazed tiles. Their cross section is either square, round, hexagonal, octagonal or 12-sided. Their form is of tower, pavilion, with multi-eaves, in the shape of an overturned bowl, with a base of diamond seat, in the shape of flower. Some were built across a street. Their variety and function were much more diversified than those of Indian pagodas.

The Jin Dynasty (1115-1234) founded after the Liao Dynasty moved its capital to Yanjing and changed its name to Zhongdu. A number of imperial palaces and gardens were built. But the rulers were even more ardent in building temples and pagodas than the former rulers. At a time there were over 100 temples in the city. Among the most famous were the Mituo Temple, Husheng Temple, Xiangshan Temple, Sheng'an Temple, Long'en Temple, Gongde Temple, Xianglin Temple and Quer Temple of Buddhism and Yuxu Temple, Tianchang Temple, Congfu Temple and Xouzhen Temple of Taoism.

FAMOUS TEMPLES IN THE CAPITAL

In 1271 Mongol chieftain Kublai Khan (reigned between 1260 and 1294) established the Yuan Impire. He built a new city over 20 years in the northeastern suburbs of Yanjing and changed its name to Dadu. In 1279 and 1234 respectively he eliminated the Southern Song Dynasty (1127-1279) and the Jin Dynasty to bring the country under a centralized rule. Beijing replaced the previous national capitals of Chang'an (present-day Xi'an in Shaanxi Province), Luoyang and Bianliang (present-day Kaifeng in Henan Province). It remained the imperial capital for 640 years through the Ming Dynasty (1368-1644) and the Qing Dynasty (1644-1911).

During the Yuan, Ming and Qing dynasties Buddhist and Toaist temples were seen everywhere inside and outside of the city. History books note over 1,000 temples. A map of Beijing made in the Qing Dynasty marks out 1,400 side streets and 1,300 temples, almost one temple for every side street. Many temples were renovated on large scale. When the Doushuai Temple was renovated during the Yuan Dynasty, for example, a Buddha statue in an inclining posture was cast, using 54 tons of copper. Thus the temple was popularly known as the Sleeping Buddha Temple. The art of painting and sculpture reached a new height during this period. The murals in the Fahai Temple in Jingshan, colored sculptures in Dahui Temple outside the city gate of Xizhimen, the carvings on the base of the Diamond Pagoda in the Five Pagoda Temple and the giant bell in the Juesheng Temple are all master pieces of the Ming Dynasty. The Diamond Pagoda and 500 arhat statues made during the Qing Dynasty in the Biyun Temple are works of superb craftsmanship.

Taoism flourished during the Yuan Dynasty thanks to the support of the rulers. The court exempted taxes on the property of Taoist temples. Taoist followers increased in great numbers.

Taoism, a native religion of China, was founded in the 2nd century and follows the philosophy of Laozi who lived during the Spring and Autumn Period (770-476 B.C.). Taoism prospered during several periods and saw its heyday during the Yuan Dynasty. It declined rapidly during the Qing Dynasty.

Lamaism (a sect of Buddhism popular in Tibet) was promoted by the central government during the Yuan Dynasty.

During the Yuan, Ming and Qing dynasties various religions including Buddhism, Taoism, Lamaism and Islamism coexisted in China. A Catholic church was built in Beijing during the Yuan Dynasty.

Temples built during the Yuan Dynasty were the most magnificent. The Tianchang Temple changed its name to Changchun Palace and underwent a grand renovation over 20 years by an imperial decree. The Dongyue Rensheng Palace, built in 1322, was the largest Taoist temple of Zhengyi sect in North China.

During the Ming Dynasty four famous mosques were renovated or built. They are the mosques on Niujie Street, Dongsi, Andingmen and Jinshifang Street.

Among the several famous Lamaist temples built during the Qing Dynasty Yonghegong is the most majestic. It used to be the residence of Emperor Yong Zheng (reigned between 1723 and 1735) before he ascended the throne. The Lamaist temple after renovation looked like an imperial palace. The East and West Huang Temples outside the city gate of Andingmen and Zongjing Dazhao Temple at Fragrant Hill in the western suburbs show a combination of the architectural styles of central China, Tibet and India.

Buddhism declined rapidly in modern times. Due to wars and neglect, the number of temples in the Beijing area decreased. Still Beijing has more temples than any other city. Ancient pagodas and temples are found among new high rise buildings, by modern overpasses or on mountain slopes. Beijing is like a museum of temples built through a period of 1,500 years. In the past decade, some temples have been turned into museums such as the Ancient Bell Museum in the Giant Bell Temple, Stela Exhibition Hall in the Zhengjue Temple, Scriptures Exhibition Hall in the Yunju Temple, Art Museum in the Wanshou Temple and Commercial Museum in the Baoguo Temple.

Ancient temples in Beijing, like the Palace Museum, the Great Wall and the Ming Tombs, are a part of the brilliant cultural heritage of the Chinese nation. Their value and function have long surpassed the original intention of the builders. These temples are grounds for religious activities and also serve as objective material for the research of architecture, sculpture, painting, literature and folklore. Tourists can enjoy their beauty and recall their long history. Temple fairs and color religious festivals make the life in Beijing livelier.

潭柘寺
THE TANZHE TEMPLE

建于1600多年前的潭柘寺是中国最古老的佛寺之一。建寺时初名嘉福寺，后多次易名，先后名龙泉寺、大万寿寺，公元1692年改称岫云寺，从此未变。由于寺后有一泓潭水，山上有一片柘林，源于二景的潭柘寺名广为流传；而岫云之名却鲜为人知。

寺建成后，历代曾多次修缮、扩建，至十七世纪末形成现在的规模。

全寺占地面积6.8公顷，分为三路，主要佛殿居中；东路为寺中高僧居处和皇族贵宾留宿的行宫院；西路是几座散落的经院和佛殿。除主要建筑外，还有位于山门外山坡上的上、下塔院和建于后山的少师静室、歇心亭，以及龙潭、御碑等。

The Tanzhe Temple built 1,600 years ago is one of China's oldest Buddhist sanctuaries. First it was named Jafu and changed to Longquan, Dawanshou and other names several times later. In 1692 it was renamed Youyun which has lasted until today. There is a pool behind the temple and a grove of three-bristle cudrania trees on the nearby mountain, local people commonly call it Tanzhe (Pool and Three-bristle Cudrania).

The temple was expanded many times. The present complex of buildings was a result of renovation toward the end of the 17th century.

The entire ground of the temple covers an area of 6.8 hectares. Along the central line are prayer halls; along the east line are living quarters for high-ranking monks and royal family and court official members when they came to the temple; and along the west line are several seperate compounds and prayer halls. Outside the front gate on the mountainslope are the Upper and Lower Pagoda Compounds, Shaoshi Meditation Room, Heart-Rest Pavilion and a stone tablet with an imperial inscription by the Dragon Pool.

潭柘寺全景 寺后翠色山峦名宝珠峰，其后九峰环列，形成“九龙戏珠”之势。

The Tanzhe Temple Behind the temple is Precious Pearl Peak, behind which in a semi-circle are eight other peaks.

大雄宝殿 佛寺中供奉释迦牟尼的主殿，一般建于寺内显要位置。潭柘寺的大雄宝殿位于天王殿后，高约 24 米，面阔约 33 米，纵宽 20 米，建于两米多高的白石台基上，巍峨高峻，为寺内诸殿之冠。

Daxiong Hall The Daxiong Hall is the main hall for worshipping Sakyamuni. It is usually located in a conspicuous spot in a temple. The Daxiong Hall in the Tanzhe Temple behind the Heavenly Kings' Hall is 24 meters high, 33 meters wide and 20 meters deep. Sitting on a white stone terrace, it is the highest structure in the temple.

释迦牟尼塑像　释迦牟尼为佛教的创始人，立于殿正中。分侍左右的立像，为其弟子阿难和迦叶。

Statue of Sakyamuni　Standing by his side are Sakyamuni's two disciples: Kasyapa and Ananda.

毗卢遮那佛 为毗卢阁内的主佛。毗卢遮那是梵文佛名，意即“光明遍照”，所以又名大日如来。佛经认为大日如来具有五种智慧，为了教化众生，化成五佛：中央大日如来佛、东方阿閦佛、南方宝生佛、西方阿弥陀佛、北方不空成就佛，毗卢阁所供即此五佛。

Vairocana The main god worshipped in the Vairocana Tower is theFirst Dhyani Buddha, all-pervasive like the light of the sun. Buddhism believes this god possesses five wisdoms which change into five Buddhas to educate people: Central Buddha of the “Great Sun”, Eastern Buddha of “Stability”, Southern Buddha of the “Source of Treasures”, Western Buddha of “Immeasurable Splendour” and Northern Buddha of the”Infallible Wise”.

毗卢阁 中路的最后一座殿阁，登阁可览全寺。阁高 16 米，面阔 33 米，分上、下两层，下层内供列 5 尊佛像。

Vairocana Tower It is last building along the central line in the temple. One can have a good view of the temple from the top of the tower. The tower is 16 meters high, 33 meters wide and of two stories. There are five Buddhist statues in the lower part.

观音菩萨像 供于寺中西北观音殿内。观音，亦名观世音。佛经称，众生倘遇危难，只需默念他的名号即能获救。据说观音为普救众生，可应机幻化三十三种形象。中国大部分佛寺所供观音，都塑绘成面容慈善的女性。

Statue of Avalokitesvara This god in the Avalokitesvara Hall in northwestern part of the temple is believed to be the God of Mercy. In distress people can solicit his help by chanting his name. He can change into 33 forms of life. Statues of Avalokitesvara in most of temples in China, however, is represented as a gracious female.

石鱼 悬于龙王殿廊下，用含铜量较高的石块雕成，重 50 公斤，长 1 米余，敲击不同的部位，可发出音阶不同的声音。传说敲击石鱼还可以遇旱化雨，祛病除疾。

Stone Fish The stone fish suspended under the eave of the Dragon King Hall was carved out of a piece of stone with high content of copper. It weighs 50 kilograms and is one meter long. Each spot emits a different scale of sound when struck. Legend has it that it has the power to get rain when it is in drought and expel illnesses.

塔院一角 山门外的山坡上，建有上、下塔院，现留存墓塔 75 座，是近千年来寺中高僧、住持的墓塔。但是，其中独有一座墓主是位公主，即元世祖忽必烈的女儿妙严，她笃信佛教，曾在寺中落发修行，圆寂后遂于塔院建塔安葬。

Pagoda Compounds In the Upper and Lower Pagoda Compounds on the slope outside the front gate there are 75 stupas in which remains of high-ranking monks are kept. Among them is a tomb of Miaozhen, a daughter of Kublai Khan of the Yuan Dynasty. She was a devoted Buddhist and became a nun in the Tanzhe Temple.

红 螺 寺
THE HONGLUO TEMPLE

位于北京北郊怀柔县境内，距市区 57 公里。寺院始建于公元 348 年，原名大明寺，明正统年间（公元 1436—1449 年）改名为护国资福禅寺。传说很久以前，寺后山巅潭中有二螺，体大色红，夕放异光，村人视为神异之物，遂将山和寺名之为“红螺”。

全寺共有五座院落，以中院为对称轴，横列于红螺山麓。主要殿堂建于中院，由南至北有山门、天王殿、大雄宝殿、三圣殿，两侧分列配殿四座；东、西两院分别为客房、厨房和方丈退居寮及供游方僧暂住的十方堂；东院旁另有一院落，是退居老僧的颐养处，名延寿堂；寺的最西部为塔院。

在历史上，红螺寺曾是中国佛教宗派之一净土宗的重要道场，慕名前来求经参拜的高僧常年不绝。该宗历代祖师共十三位，而成道于红螺寺的竟有两位。

红螺寺之所以闻名，还因为它是北方重要的气功传习地，至今寺中尚存有当年气功练习场遗址。

红螺寺远眺　寺背倚红螺山，前有凤凰山为屏，青龙山与白虎岗峙立东西，构成了一幅“深山藏古寺”的画境。

The Hongluo Temple Behind the temple is Hongluo Mountain, in front of it is Fenghuang Mountain, to its east is Qinglong Mountain and to its west is Baihu Hill.

The Hongluo Temple is located in Huairou County 57 kilometers from the city proper. It was built in 348 A.D. and named Daming. Between 1336 and 1449 it was renamed Huguo Zifu. A story tells that in ancient times two huge red spiral shells lived in a pond behind the temple and emitted strange light. Villagers thus began to call the mountain on which the temple stands and the temple Hongluo (Red Spiral Shell).

The temple's five compounds are arranged up Hongluo Mountain. From south to north there are the front gate, Heavenly King Hall, Daxiong Hall and Three-Sages Hall. There are also wing halls. The eastern and western compounds have guest rooms, kitchen, abbbot's living quarter and rooms for visiting monks. Beside the eastern compound a small courtyard is the living quarters for retired monks. The stupas are located in a compound to the far west.

The Hongluo Temple was once an important place of the Pure Land sect of Buddhism. Among the 13 high monks of the sect, two died in this temple.

The Hongluo Temple is famous because it is a major ground to teach qigong (breath excercise).

山门 寺院依山而筑，高低有致。从寺前牌坊至山门，地势渐趋升高，山门建于高坡之上，门额上嵌有"护国资福禅寺"题匾。

The front gate The terrain begins to rise from an archway to the front gate. On the plaque is its official name: "Huguo Zifu".

天王殿内景　弥勒佛居中而坐，两侧分立四大天王。

Inside the Heavenly King Hall Maitreya Buddha is seated in the middle with four Heavenly Kings standing on his either side.

大雄宝殿外景 殿为单檐庑殿式建筑，宽五间。殿前有雌雄银杏树各一株，高约 30 米，树龄逾千年。雌树不开花，而秋季果实累累；雄树每至春季繁花满枝，却不结果。此二树与山门前的万竿翠竹及主殿后的绕松紫藤，并称为寺中三绝。

Outside the Daxiong Hall Two ginkgo trees in front of the palatial hall are 30 meters high and over 1,000 years old. The female tree does not bloom but bears fruit in autumn. The male tree blooms in spring but does not bear fruit. The two trees, a bamboo grove and purple vines around pine trees behind the main hall are "three wonders" of the temple.

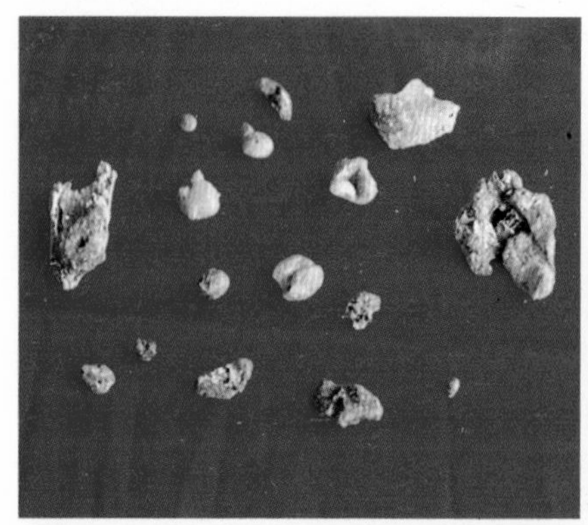

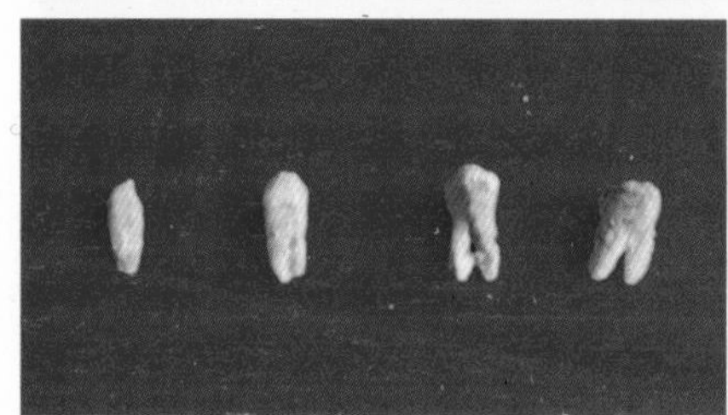

际醒祖师舍利塔 位于寺西塔院内。际醒祖师（公元 1741－1810 年），清代高僧、净土宗第十二位祖师，曾在红螺寺弘扬净土宗经法，70 岁时圆寂于寺内。大师遗体火化后，获舍利子百余粒，葬于此塔下。另图为际醒大师的部分牙齿和舍利子。

Stupa of High Monk Jixing The stupa in the Stupa Compound keeps more than 100 beads of granulated ashes of High Monk Jixing under it. Monk Jixing (1741-1810) was the 12th Master of the Pure Land sect. He propogated the sect teachings in the Hongluo Temple and died there at the age of 70. The other picture shows some of his teeth and granulated ashes.

天　宁　寺
THE TIANNING TEMPLE

天宁寺的前身是北魏延兴年间（公元471－476年）所建的光林寺，自建成至今寺宇屡毁屡建，名称先后改为弘业寺、天王寺、大万安禅寺，公元1435年定为今名。

天宁寺现存建筑，以寺后佛塔最为壮观。塔总高57.8米，为砖筑实心密檐式八角塔，造型庄重秀丽。寺塔建于十二世纪辽代，当时它矗立于辽都燕京内城之东，是城内屈指可数的高大建筑。

寺自建成至今已经八个多世纪，其间北京城区位置几经变迁，范围不断拓宽，天宁寺现居市区西南广安门外，以天宁寺命名的立交桥凌架于寺的侧畔，这里已成为北京颇具特色的街景之一。

The Tianning Temple was built on the site of the Guanlin Temple which was built between 471 and 476 in the Northern Wei Dynasty. It was destroyed many times and its name was changed to Hongyue, Tianwang and Dawan'an. The present name was given in 1435.

Among the extant structures the most majestic is a pagoda behind the temple. It is 57.8 meters high, solid of bricks, octagonal and with multi-layers of eaves. The pagoda was built in the 12th century during the Liao Dynasty, one of a few high buildings of the time.

Since the construction of the Tianning Temple more than 800 years ago, the location of Beijing city has constantly altered and expanded. The temple has been enclosed in the city proper to the southwest today. A modern overpass rises majestically by it.

天宁寺塔　塔由须弥座、塔身、十三层密檐和塔刹组成，各部分疏密、繁简配置得当，极富韵律感。

The Pagoda of the Tianning Temple
The graceful pagoda is composed of the Sumeru base, the body, 13 tiers of eaves and the crown.

塔身雕刻 雕有佛像、菩萨以及仿木结构的门窗、斗拱、椽柱，均精细逼真。

Carvings on the Pagoda Buddhist statues and brick windows, doors, rafters and pillars in imitation of wood are vividly carved in relief.

北魏太和造像

STONE BUDDHIST STATUE OF THE NORTHERN WEI DYNASTY

为一石雕佛像，造于北魏太和十三年（公元 489 年），是北京现存最古老的佛教雕像。石像立于今北京海淀温泉车儿营村，此处原有一座寺庙，名石佛寺，石像是寺中主佛，因年代久远寺已无存。

石像高 2.2 米，据说是仿照魏孝文帝的身量、形貌雕造的。孝文帝名拓跋宏（公元 471–499 年在位）是北魏的第七位皇帝。北魏皇室原是生活在中国北方的鲜卑族的一支，孝文帝入主帝位后曾颁发多项政令，以促进鲜卑族与汉族及其它民族的融合，因而受到尊崇。

石像背面雕有多尊小佛像，背光上刻有精致的纹饰和十余尊手持乐器的伎乐飞天。

The statue carved in the 13th year of the Taihe period (489) during the Northern Wei Dynasty is the oldest Buddhist statue in the Beijing area. It stands at Cherying Village in Wenquan, Haidian District. There used to be a temple named Stone Buddha.

The statue is housed in a hexagonal stone room. It is said it is a copy of the real person of Emperor Xiao Wen of the Northern Wei Dynasty. Emperor Xiao Wen (Tuoba Hong, reigned between 471 and 499) was the seventh emperor of the Northern Wei Dynasty. The royal family used to be a part of the Xianbei nationality in north China. Emperor Xiao Wen issued many decrees to encourage his people to assimilate the culture of other nationalities. This ruler was highly respected.

There are many smaller Buddha statues on the back of the gigantic statue and fine designs and a dozen flying Apsara musicians on the halo.

小坐像 雕于魏太和造像的背面，象征辅佐帝王的群臣。

Smaller Buddha Statues They represent court officials assisting the emperor.

魏太和造像 其面部圆润丰满，神态自若，显现出帝王之尊。

Buddha Statue of the Northern Wei
The plumpy face and easy expression show the dignity of an emperor.

云 居 寺
THE YUNJU TEMPLE

又名西峪寺，位于北京西南郊石经山西麓，距城 75 公里。

云居寺始建于七世纪初，由于历代不断增建，殿堂布局严整，构筑崇丽，成为驰誉京城的名刹之一。寺的中部六座主殿自东而西排列有序，左右两侧的重重院落为僧舍、客房和行宫。寺中大部分建筑于本世纪三十年代毁于战火，仅存古塔、碑刻。数年前开始重建，现已初具规模。

云居寺之所以闻名，还因寺外石经山中和寺南侧塔下藏有历经千年刻就的石经版 14278 石，为中国佛教经籍铭刻之最。1992 年评出的“十大北京旅游世界之最”中，云居寺即是其一，被称为世界上收藏石刻经版最多的寺庙。

Also known as the Xiyu Temple, the Yunju Temple is located on the western side of Shijing Mountain in the southwestern suburbs of Beijing, 75 kilometers from the city proper.

Construction of the temple began during the seventh century. It was constantly expanded during later dynasties. The grand temple is among the most famous Buddhist sanctuaries in the Beijing area. Six main halls are arranged from east to west. Courtyards on both sides are living quarters and guest rooms. Most of the buildings were destroyed during the war in the 1930s. Today only a pagoda and inscriptions on stone tablets were left. Reconstruction that began several years ago has restored much of its original splendour.

The temple became famous for the 14,278 stone slabs bearing Buddhist scriptures carved over 1,000 years. They are kept in caves in Shijing (Stone Scripture) Mountain and under the pagoda. The temple was selected as one of the "top ten of tourist world in Beijing" in 1992. It has the largest number of scriptures carved on stone in the world.

藏经洞　石经山中凿有九个石洞，共藏石经版 4196 块，九洞中除雷音洞可进入外，其余八洞皆以石门锢封。图为藏经洞外景。

Vaults for Keeping Buddhist Scriptures There are 4,196 pieces of stone with inscriptions of Buddhist scriptures kept in nine caves on Shijing Mountain. Only the Leiyin Cave is open to visitors. The other eight are still sealed with stone. This is outside the Leiyin Cave.

雷音洞 又名华严堂、石经堂，开凿于七世纪初，四壁嵌有静琬法师最初镌刻的石经版 146 块。洞中四根八棱形石柱上雕刻佛像一千余尊，人称千佛柱。

The Leiyin Cave Also known as Huayan Hall and Shijing Hall, the cave was dug in the early seventh century. Inlaid on its walls there are the earliest 146 stone slabs with Buddhist scriptures carved by Monk Jingwan. Four octagonal stone pillars bear relief carvings of more than 1,000 Buddha statues.

石经库一角 建于 1980 年，发掘出的石经版皆按序号存于此。

Stone Scripture Slabs They are displayed in an exhibition hall built in 1980.

观音立像 立于大悲殿正中，此殿为寺中路最后一座殿堂。

Standing Statue of Avalokitesvara
It is housed in the Dabei Hall, the last hall along the central line of the temple.

北塔　云居寺南北两侧原有两塔对峙，南塔早毁，此为北塔。塔的下部为楼阁式，上部为覆钵式。该塔初建于公元 711 年，经后代重修，成此造型。

Northern Pagoda　Two pagodas used to stand on the northern and southern side of the Yunju Temple. The southern one was destroyed a long time ago. The lower part of the Northern Pagoda is in the style of a Chinese traditional tower and the upper part looks like an overturned bowl. It was first built in 711 and underwent repairs and renovations many times.

唐代浮雕 北塔四周有建于公元八世纪初的唐代石塔四座，内外皆刻有纹饰和题记，图为塔龛中的浮雕佛像与胁侍，其线条柔美，形体丰腴，正是唐代风格。

Buddha Niches Four stone pagodas stand around the Northern Pagoda built in the early eighth century during the Tang Dynasty. They bear inscriptions and designs. The picture shows a Buddha statue and Buddha attendants in relief in typical Tang Dynasty style of flowy lines and plumpy posture.

唐塔 人称金仙公主塔，公主为唐玄宗（公元 712-756 年在位）第八妹，因她曾奏请其兄赐予云居寺经本、土地、山林，故公元 731 年寺僧建塔以志之。

Tang Dynasty Pagoda The pagoda was built in 731 by the monks in memory of Princess Jinxian, eighth sister of Emperor Xuan Zong of the Tang Dynasty (reigned between 712 and 756). The princess asked his emperor brother to allocate Buddhist scriptures, land and trees to the Yunju Temple.

鸟瞰云居寺 寺后为石经山，因山腰常有白云缭绕，故原名白带山，后因山中藏有石经版，改为今名。

The Yunju Temple Behind the temple is Shijing Mountain. It was originally called White Belt Mountain because white clouds often appear in the middle of it. It changed to present name because the mountain keeps scriptures carved on stone.

西山八大处
BADACHU (EIGHT GRAND SIGHTS)

北京西郊，一座重峦复冈的山脉由西北绵延至西南，这就是被称之为京华右臂的西山。西山多胜景，尤多古寺，西山八大处统指位居一支皋上的八座寺庙。

在西山一条支皋的东麓，环立着三座青峰：翠微山、平坡山和卢师山。三山上下，林茂花香，泉冽石奇，四季皆有美景佳趣，其间分布有八座古刹，人们遂以“三山八刹十二景”概括此处景物。

八大处的八座寺院分别是：一处长安寺、二处灵光寺、三处三山庵、四处大悲寺、五处龙王堂、六处香界寺、七处宝珠洞、八处证果寺。

八寺于公元七世纪至十七世纪间陆续创建。各寺布局因所据山势而异，寺中建筑、景物各具特色，或以塔闻名，或以雕塑称绝，或以林泉和洞窟奇幽取胜。各寺之间均有路、桥相通。

The Western Mountains run from northwest to southwest in the western suburbs of Beijing. Among the many ancient temples in the mountains eight are the best known at Badachu.

Three mountains, Cuiwei, Pingbo and Lushi, rise in a semi circle on the eastern side of the Western Mountains. The eight temples are located among dense woods and cool springs in these mountains. They have been tourist attractions for a long time for their long history and pleasant surroundings.

The eight temples are named Chang'an, Lingguang, Sanshan, Dabei, Longwang, Xiangjie, Baozhudong and Zhengguo. They were built between the seventh century to the 17th century. Each has its particular features. Some are known for their pagodas, some for their sculptures, some for their trees and springs and still some for their mysterious caves. The temples are about one kilometer apart and connected by roads and bridges.

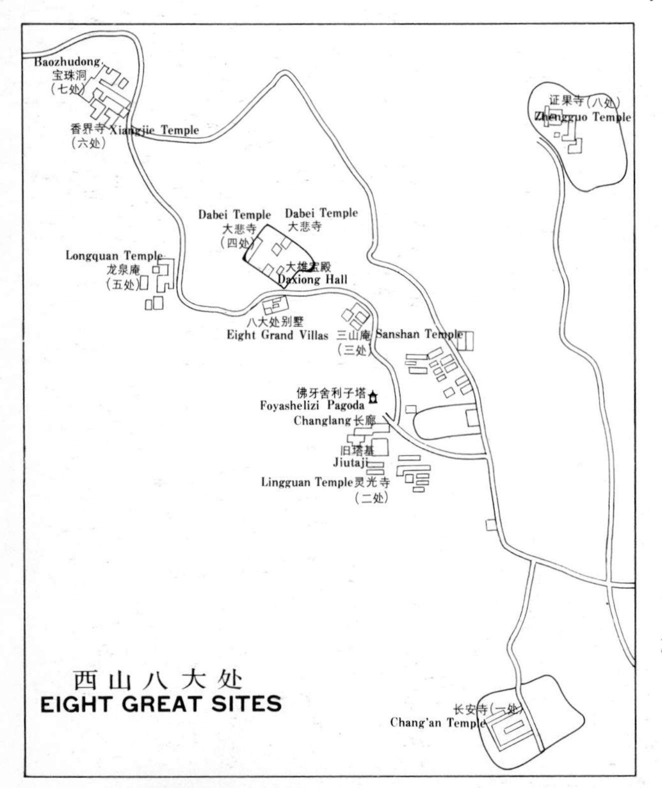

八大处寺庙分布示意图

A SKETCH MAP OF EIGHT TEMPLES AT BADACHU

灵光寺 建于八世纪下半叶，为八大处第二处。此寺初名龙泉寺，公元 1478 年改为今名。图为寺中庭院之一，池中饲有各色金鱼，最大的长达 70 厘米，相传清咸丰年间（公元 1851–1861 年）始养金鱼，迄今已百余年。

The Lingguang Temple When it was built in the latter half of the eighth century it was named Longquan. The present name was given in 1478. The picture shows a pool in the compound with gold fish. It is said the pool began to have gold fish 100 years ago. The largest ones measure 70 centimeters.

古银杏　生长于大悲寺一庭院中，年逾 800 多年，仍枝荣叶茂，为八大处一绝。

Ancient Ginkgo Tree　The 800 year-old tree in the compound of the Dabei Temple still flourishes.

龙王堂一景——龙泉　龙王堂以泉著称。泉水从寺后峭壁下蜿蜒流入池内，池后的殿堂中供有龙王塑像。

Dragon Fountain　The Longwang (Dragon King) Hall is famous for a fountain behind the temple. A statue of the Dragon King is worshipped in a hall by the pool.

碑石 立于香界寺内，碑上所刻大悲观音像为唇下生髭的男性形象，据此，专家认为碑是唐代遗物。

Stone Stele Unearthed in 1678, the stone tablet kept at the Xiangjie Temple has a portrait of Avalokitesvara. It is described as a male with a beard. Specialists believe the portrait was made during the Tang Dynasty because in later times the god was usually represented as a female.

香界寺 为八大处的主要寺院，古代帝王游山降香，必到此休息。寺依平坡山而建，五重殿宇，层层递升。图为山门内寺景。

The Xiangjie Temple It is the most important temple among the eight temples at Badachu. When emperors came to Badachu they would take a rest in the temple. Five main halls are arranged on the mountain slope. This is a scene just inside the front gate.

宝珠洞寺 位于平坡山极顶，图为寺前牌坊。

'The Baozhudong Temple It stands on the top of Pingpo Mountain. The picture shows an archway in front of the front gate.

证果寺秘摩崖 相传七世纪初，一卢姓和尚自江南乘舟飘流至此崖下，遂入石室中修行。龙王之子幻化为二童子拜他为师。后来当地遇旱，两童子施法降雨，而后化作双龙乘云而去。人们为感念师徒三人，建寺于山上。

The Mimo Crag of the Zhengguo Temple Legend has it that in the early seventh century a monk named Lu came here from the south of the Yangtze River and began meditation in a stone room under the crag. Two sons of the Dragon King changed into the form of human beings to learn Buddhism from Monk Lu. The area was hit by a drought. The two dragons brought rain and then flew away. The local people built a temple in memory of the monk and the two young dragons.

选佛场　为一重檐盝顶方形建筑，内设戒坛。

Buddha selection Ground　The multi-eave square structure houses the Ordination Terrace.

戒坛　为明代遗物，汉白玉石砌筑，高约5米，共三级，最上层设莲花宝座和释迦牟尼坐像，还摆放着明代雕花沉香木椅10把，是当年受戒时传戒师和证人僧的座位；戒坛四周神龛内有百余尊戴盔披甲、神态威武的戒神。此戒坛是中国现存戒坛中最大的一座。

The Ordination Terrace　The terrace built during the Ming Dynasty is made of white marble stone slabs over three meters high in three tiers. A statue of Sakyamuni seated on a lotus flower seat is on the upper tier. There are also ten chairs of agalloch eaglewood on the upper tier used in old times by the preacher and witnesses on ordination. Around the terrace stand 100 armored guardians in niches. This ordination terrace is the largest of its kind in China.

辽塔　建于寺内东北塔院，左塔为辽代高僧法均的墓塔，右为普贤衣钵塔。

The Liao Dynasty Pagodas　They are located in the Pagoda Compound in the northeastern part of the temple. The one on the left keeps the remains of Monk Fajun of the Liao Dynasty and the one on the right keeps the clothes and alms bowl of Monk Puxian.

卧龙松 植于辽代，为戒台寺诸松之首。此松扎根于石砌的高墙上，凌空横卧，虬曲离奇，有如苍龙倚碑石而息。碑刻"卧龙松"三字为清代恭亲王奕䜣所书。

Inclining Dragon Pine Planted during the Liao Dynasty, the tree is the leader of the pine trees in the Jetai Temple. Its roots are deep in a stone wall and its branches stretch horizontally like a dragon. The three characters meaning inclining dragon pine is in the handwriting of Prince Yi Xin of the Qing Dynasty.

九龙松 形态高大，气势磅礴，主干分九杈，仿佛九龙腾绕，故名九龙松。

Nine-Dragon Pine The giant pine tree has nine main branches spreading out like nine flying dragons, thus its name.

卧 佛 寺
WOFO (SLEEPING BUDDHA) TEMPLE

卧佛寺位于北京市西北郊寿安山南麓，距城约 20 公里。

寺始建于七世纪前半叶，初名兜率寺。以后屡废屡建，寺名亦屡易，先后名寿安山寺、大昭孝寺、洪庆寺、永安寺等。公元 1734 年清代皇室又一次重建并赐名十方普觉寺。早在建寺之初，寺内就供有檀木雕卧佛像，公元 1321 年又铸造了一尊巨型释迦牟尼铜卧佛供于寺中，因此，人皆称其卧佛寺，历代帝王所赐的诸多正名反而极少被人提及。

卧佛寺的建筑格局，仍保留着中国早期佛寺的遗制，以山门、天王殿、三世佛殿、卧佛殿为中轴，由南平展至北，两侧环以配殿、廊庑，将四重殿宇联为一体。寺院东、西两路是行宫、僧舍，与主体建筑以墙相隔。里面庭院重重，点缀着荷池、山石花木，别是一番景趣。

The Wofo Temple lies in the northwestern suburbs of Beijing, 20 kilometers from the city proper.

Built in the first half of the seventh century, it was first named Doushuai. The temple was collapsed and rebuilt several times and the name changed to Shou'an, Dazhaoxiao, Hongqing and Yong'an. In 1734 the imperial court of the Qing Dynasty rebuilt the temple and named it Shifang Pujue. Through its history there had been a Buddha statue of sandalwood in an inclining posture. In 1321 a copper statue of Sakyamuni, also in an inclining posture, was cast. From then on people began to call it Sleeping Buddha Temple.

The layout of the temple has retained much influence of the Buddhist temples in the early days. Along the central axisfrom south to north are the front gate, Heavenly Kings Hall, the Hall of Trikala Buddhas and the Hall of the Sleeping Buddha. Wing halls and roofed corridors enclose the four halls. Seperated by walls on the east and west side are houses where monks used to live in and temperory living quarters for royal family members and court officials when they visited the temple. The several courtyards are decorated with lotus flower ponds, artificial rockeries, flowers and trees.

铜卧佛 身长 5.2 余米，重 25 吨，头西足东，面南而卧；像的东、西、北三面环立 12 尊高 1.2 米的彩色泥塑像。据传这组佛像表现了释迦牟尼临终时向十二位弟子嘱咐后事的情景。

Copper Sleeping Buddha The Buddha in an inclining posture is 5.3 meters long and weighs 54 tons. It lies on a couch facing the south with the head toward the west. Twelve colored clay statues of 1.2 meters high stand on the east, west and north around it. It is said this is the scene when Sakyamuni was giving his last words to his 12 disciples at the death bed.

琉璃牌坊　穿过牌坊，便进入宝刹胜境。

Glazed Tile Archway　This archway serves as the first entrance to the temple.

三世佛殿 寺内第二重殿堂，内供三世佛，其两侧供列十八罗汉像。

The Hall of Trikala Buddhas The second hall of the temple houses the Trikala Buddhas and 18 Arhats.

法源寺
THE FAYUAN TEMPLE

位于市区西南宣武门外，是北京市内现存历史最悠久的寺庙之一。

法源寺的前身悯忠寺自公元696年建成至十五世纪，近千年间曾先后毁于火灾、兵燹，由于寺为国中巨刹，所以每次废圮之后，旋又修复，而且比前更加恢宏壮丽。公元1442年重建后改名为崇福寺。今日寺院的规模和布局即是那时形成的。

十七、十八世纪，清代的几位帝王屡次敕令在寺中建坛造阁，1733年又重加修缮，并改名法源寺。

法源寺的布局与卧佛寺颇相似。在南北中轴线上建有六座主要殿堂，四周围以配殿和廊庑，形成了南北长180余米、东西宽50米的封闭式殿庭。东西庑外侧为僧舍。

中国佛学院设于寺内。

四大天王像 立于天王殿，是十五世纪的遗存。像高1.2米，用青铜铸成，较之其它寺中的泥塑彩像更加威武。

The Fayuan Temple, one of the oldest in the Beijing area, is located outside the Xuanwu city gate in the southwestern part of Beijing.

The Minzhong Temple, predecessor of the Fayuan, was built in 696. It was destroyed by fire and war several times in a period of 1,000 years. Because it was an important temple, the central government always reuilt it and made it more magnificent. In 1442, after a large-scale renovation, it was renamed the Congfu Temple. The present temple has retained the scale of that time.

During the 17th and 18th centuries, emperors of the Qing Dynasty ordered halls and towers be built in the temple and changed its name to Fayuan.

The layout of the Fayuan Temple is much similar to that of the Wofo Temple: six main halls are arranged along the central axis with wing halls and covered corridors around them. The temple is 180 meters from south to north and 50 meters from east to west, enclosed by a wall. Wing houses on the eastern and western side were living quarters of monks.

The temple today houses China Buddhist Institute.

Statues of the Four Heavenly Kings
The Hall of the Four Heavenly Kings (Buddha's warrior attendants) was built in the 15th century. The four bronze tatues are 1.2 meters high, looking more awesome than those made of colored clay.

悯忠台 建于悯忠阁遗址，里面陈列着历代石函、经幢、刻石等。

The Minzhong Terrace The terrace was built on the site of the Minzhong Tower. On display inside are stone boxes, pillars inscribed with scriptures and stone carvings.

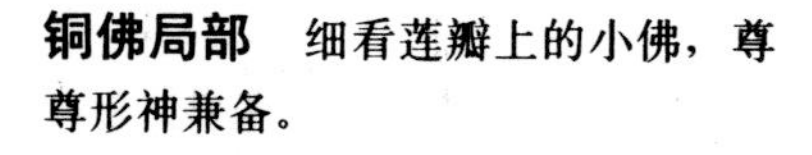

铜佛局部　细看莲瓣上的小佛，尊尊形神兼备。

Detail of the Copper Buddha Statues
The small statues of Buddha look life like.

铜佛　明代铸造，供奉于毗卢殿内，像通高 4.58 米，共三层。法身佛毗卢遮那居于顶层；四方佛居中层，分别面向四方；下层为千瓣莲花宝座，每一莲瓣上刻有一尊小佛，表示诸化身佛环绕佛的法身。

Copper Buddha Statues　Cast during the Ming Dynasty, the statues in the Hall of Vairocana as a group are 4.58 meters high in three tiers. The upper part is Vairocana (First Dhyani Buddha), the middle part is the Four Direction Buddhas each facing a direction and the lower part is a lotus flower seat. On each petal of the flower is a small statue of Buddha.

木雕佛像 供于藏经阁下层，为明代遗物，佛像长 7.4 米。

Wooden Statue of Buddha The statue in the lower part of the Scripture Library was made in the Ming Dynasty. It is 7.4 meters long. The upper part of the tower keeps Buddhist statues of the Ming Dynasty and scriptures made during the Ming and Qing dynasties.

藏经阁 建于静寂的后院，须从大悲坛两侧穿门过院，几经曲折方可抵达阁前。

Scripture Library The library is located in the quiet back yard of the temple. It can be reached only through side doors of the Dabei Hall.

自在观音铜像 供奉于大悲坛，像的姿态舒展，神情恬适。

Copper Carefree Avalokitesvara It is housed in the Dabei Hall.

白 云 观
THE BAIYUN (WHITE CLOUD) TEMPLE

白云观是北京著名的道观，位于横贯市区中部的通衢长安街西段南侧。

观初建于公元 739 年，原名天长观，公元 1203 年改名太极宫。十三世纪二十年代元太祖成吉思汗命道士丘处机（公元 1148－1227 年）掌管全国道教，并任太极宫住持，因为丘处机道号长春子，所以宫于公元 1227 年更名为长春宫。十四世纪末观毁于兵火，十五世纪初明皇室敕令重建，始成今日规模，并定名白云观。

全观建筑分为中、东、西三路及后院四部分，面积 1 万多平方米。中路由南至北排列六座主殿，配殿和廊庑分列两旁。东、西两路配置多座独立而又相通的院落，内建斋堂、塔和小型殿堂。后院名云集园，建于公元 1887 年，内建楼、亭、台、馆，环以长廊，遍植花木，是一处别致的园林式建筑。

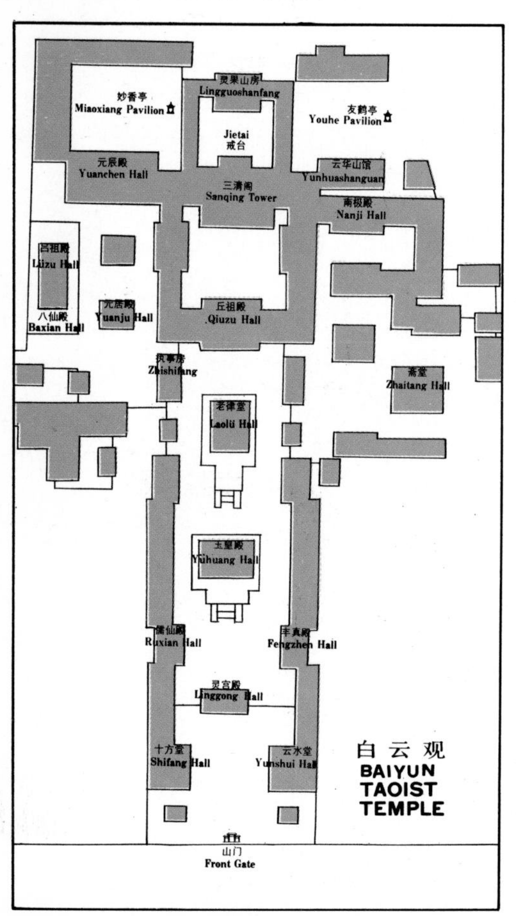

The famous Taoist temple in the Beijing area is located toward the western end of Chang'an Boulevard which runs through the middle of Beijing from east to west.

It was named Tianchang when it was first built in 739 and renamed Taiji Palace in 1203. In the 1320s Ganghis Khan of the Yuan Dynasty put Qiu Chuji (1148-1227) in charge of Taoist affairs of the country and named him abbot of the Taijing Palace. Qu Chuji was also known as Changchun Zi. So the temple was renamed Changchun Palace in 1227. The temple was destroyed during a war at the end of the 14th century. In the 15th century the imperial court of the Ming Dynasty ordered the temple be rebuilt and renamed Baiyun, or White Cloud.

The whole complex is divided into the central, eastern and western routes and the back yard, covering an area of 10,000 square meters. The central route has the six main halls from south to north with wing halls and roofed corridors on both sides. On the eastern and western routes are independent but connected courtyards with fast halls, pagodas and smaller prayer halls. Yunji Garden, the back yard, built in 1887, has atower, pavilion, terrace, long corridor and many flowering plants.

山门 建于明代，为面阔三间的歇山式建筑，三洞拱形门象征道教“三界”（即所谓欲界、色界、无色界），门前有华表、石狮，门内东西各竖旗杆一根，悬黄龙旗幡，东幡书“国泰民安”，西幡题“风调雨顺”。

Front Gate Built during the Ming Dynasty, the front gate has three openings signifying the “three worlds” of Taoism: the world of desire, the world of substance and the world of non-substance. In front of the gate are decorative pillars and stone lions. Inside the gate are two flag poles on each side with yellow flags with a partern of dragon. On the eastern flag are written “National peace and secure life”, and on the western flag are written “Soft wind and benificial rain”.

牌坊 为四柱七楼木结构，匾额正面书“洞天胜境”，背面书“琼琳阆苑”。

Archway The wooden archway is composed of four pillars and seven tiers. On the front of the plaque are the characters meaning “Holy Land of Heavenly Cave,” and on the back of the plaque are the characters meaning “Garden of Jade”.

老子雕像 老子为道教创始人，相传此尊雕像是公元 739 年道观初建时唐玄宗所赐。

Statue of Lao Zi Lao Zi (Li Er) is the founder of Taoism. It is said this statue was given to the temple by Emperor Xuan Zong of the Tang Dynasty in 739 when the temple was built.

老律堂 是道教全真龙门派历代律师传戒说法的殿堂，内部开阔，是观内进行宗教活动的主要场所。堂前有一头铜铸骡子。这头铜骡不仅形象逼真，民间传说，它还能祛病免灾，无论何人，只要诚心诚意告之病痛，并抚摸它的相应部位，病即可除。

The Hall of Lao Lu This is a hall where preachers of the All Truth Dragon Gate Sect of Taoism gave lectures. The expansive hall is the main place of religious service. There is a copper donkey in front of the hall. Folk tales say the donkey has the power to expel illnesses. One may tell it his or her illness or touch the part of the donkey responding to the part of his or her body where he or she feels ill, the illness will go away.

老律堂内的法事活动
A Service in the Hall of Lao Lu.

丘祖殿　建于金正大五年（公元1228年），初名“处顺堂”，殿为三开间，是全真龙门派后裔奉祀丘处机的殿堂，堂下埋藏丘祖遗蜕。清康熙年间改名“贞寂堂”，乾隆四十五年（公元1780年）改为今名。

The Hall of Master Qiu Built in 1228, the hall was first named Chushun. It is the place to worship Qiu Chuji of the All-Truth Dragon Gate Sect of Taoism. The remains of Qiu are buried under the floor of the hall. The name changed to Zhenji in the reign of Emperor Kang Xi of the Qing Dynasty. The present name was given in 1780.

丘祖殿内景 左为丘祖塑像。丘处机生于 1148 年，1227 年羽化，享年 80 岁。

Inside the Hall of Master Qiu On the left is a statue of Qiu Chuji. Qiu was born in 1148 and died in 1227 at the age of 80.

三清阁、四御殿外景　上层为三清阁，内供道教崇奉的最高天神玉清、上清、太清三天尊像；下层四御殿内供天神界的四位大帝像。

The Tower of the Pure Trinity and the Hall of Four Guardians The upper part of the Tower of the Pure Trinity houses the three highest gods of Taoism: Jade Purity, Upper Purity and Supreme Purity. The lower part houses the statues of four heavenly emperors.

铜鼎炉　立于三清阁、四御殿前，炉铸于公元 1529 年，高 1.16 米，上雕有大小游龙 38 条，三鼎足各雕有狻猊头像。

Bronze Tripod Cauldron The cauldron in front of the Tower of the Pure Trinity and the Hall of Four Guardians was cast in 1529 and is 1.16 meters high. On the outside are carved 38 swimming dragons and on the three legs are heads of lion.

大明嘉靖己丑年製

戒台 位于云集园中部。白云观中每年春秋授戒，戒期各 53 日，授受经戒皆有严格的传承规则，受戒合格者，发给戒牒，方成为道门中不同品级的弟子。

Ordination Terrace The terrace is located in the middle of the Yunji Garden. The Baiyun Temple ordinates novices in the spring and autumn every year. The ordination lasts 53 days following strict specifications. Those who have passed receive certificates and become disciples of various grades.

云集园游廊 它把云集园隔为似分犹连的三个庭院，使这处神仙洞府更加幽深隐秘。

Corridor of the Yunji Garden The garden is divided by a corridor into three sections to make the holy place more mysterious.

牛街礼拜寺
MOSQ UE ON NIUJIE STREET

北京西南城区有一条回族聚居的街道，名叫牛街。牛街礼拜寺就建在街的中段东侧，是北京地区规模最大，历史最久的一座清真寺。

牛街礼拜寺建于公元996年，寺中建筑采用中国传统的木结构形式，但是，其总体布局和细部装饰依旧保持伊斯兰的建筑特色。

主要建筑有寺门、望月楼、礼拜楼、邦克楼、碑亭及沐浴室等，总面积虽不大，但是布局紧凑，殿堂结构富有变化，雕饰华美，与佛教寺庙相比，有异曲同工之妙。

按照伊斯兰教教规，教徒作礼拜时，要面对西方朝拜圣地麦加，因而寺门坐东朝西，殿堂中也以西面为尊。又因《古兰经》禁止用动物形象作装饰，所以建筑的装饰纹样均为阿拉伯文字和几何图案。

Niujie Mosque, the oldest and largest mosque in the Beijing area, is located in the middle of Niujie Street inhabited by the Huis, a minority nationality of Moslem. It was built in 996.

The mosque is entirely wooden of Chinese traditional architecuture, but Islamic in appearance and decoration. Main structures are the front gate, Looking-at-the-Moon Tower, Service Hall, Bang (Summons) Hall, Stele Pavilion and bathroom. They are compactly laid out in a not very large area and richly decorated.

Moslems face the direction of Mecca in service. So the front gate faces west toward Mecca. The west side of the halls is also the most important. The Koran forbids to use animal designs as decoration. The mosque is decorated with geometrical designs or Arabic letters.

礼拜殿殿顶 为六角攒尖亭式藻井，其装饰为典型的阿拉伯图样。

Top of the Service Hall The hexagonal tapering caisson is typically decorated in Arabic style.

礼拜寺外景 寺门内的六角形楼阁即望月楼，高10余米，每年斋月开始的前一日和最后一日，由阿訇登楼观月，以决定开斋和封斋的时辰。

Outside the Mosque The hexagonal structure just inside the front gate is the Looking-at-the-Moon Tower of 10 meters high. One day before and one day after the Ramadan (the month of fast), an ahung goes up the tower to look at the moon and decides the time of the beginning and end of the month of fast.

礼拜殿内景 为寺内主要殿堂，纵深30余米，可容千人礼拜。

Inside the Service Hall The main hall in the mosque is 30 meters deep and can hold over 1,000 people.

大 觉 寺
THE DAJUE TEMPLE

北京西山群峰之中，有一座形如卧狮的山峰，名旸台山，闻名京师的大觉古寺便建在山之东坡。

寺始建于公元 1068 年，因为有一脉清泉流经全寺，故名清水院，后易名灵泉寺。公元 1428 年重修后改称大觉寺。

寺背西面东，自东入山门经石桥，依次可达天王殿、大雄宝殿、无量寿佛殿、大悲坛，直至建于山腰的舍利塔下。主要殿堂两侧建有戒坛，以及清皇室敕建的南、北玉兰院和四宜堂院等。

寺中有被誉为“大觉六绝”的奇景珍物，即千载古碑，清泉汇注的龙潭，六人方可合抱的古银杏树，植于 400 年前的白玉兰，抱塔松和用晶润如玉的巨石凿刻的水池。

Among the West Mountains in Beijing there is a peak like a crouching lion — Yangtai Mountain. The famous Dajue Temple is located on the eastern side of the mountain.

When it was built in 1068, it was named Qingquan (Clear Spring) because the water from a spring flew through the temple. The name changed to Lingquan later. The present name was given in 1428 when it was rebuilt. The temple faces east. Inside the front gate across a stone bridge and up the slope there are the Heavenly King Hall, Daxiong Hall, the Hall of Amitayus, Dabei Hall and Relics Pagoda. Flanking the main halls are ordination terraces and the South and North Yulan Compounds and Siyutang Compound.

Dajue Temple is famous for its "Six Wonders" — a 1,000-year-old stele, Dragon Pool with clear spring water, an ancient ginkgo tree that can be encircled by six people with their arms linked, magnolia trees planted 400 years ago, a pine tree wrapping a pagoda and a pond built with giant whte stone slabs.

三世佛像 供奉于大雄宝殿，佛像古朴凝重，具有十五世纪遗风。

Statues of Trikala Buddhas The statues in Daxiong Hall represent the solemn style of the 15th century.

无量寿佛殿 此殿为寺中主要建筑之一，内供西方三圣——无量寿佛及其左右胁侍观世音菩萨和大势至菩萨。

The Hall of Amitayus The main hall of the temple houses the statues of one of the Three Sages of the West — Amitayus and his two attentants — Avalokitesvara and Mahasthamaprapta.

无量寿佛 又名阿弥陀佛，为西方极乐世界教主。佛经说，此佛过去为菩萨时，曾发 48 愿，长期修行，成为佛陀。《阿弥陀经》说，念此佛名号，深信无疑，死后即能往生其净土。后世所谓“念佛”，多指念其名号——阿弥陀佛。图中左为大势至菩萨，右为观世音菩萨。

Amitayus Also known as Amitabha, it is the chief leader of the Joyful World of the West. According to Buddhist scriptures, when this Buddha was still a Bodhisattva, he made 48 pledges. According to the Amitabha Sutra, a believer will be allowed to go to the Pure Land if he or she chats the name of this Buddha. On his left is Mahasthamaprapta and on his right is Avalokitesvara.

古银杏　植于辽代，距今近千年，寺中六绝之一。

Ancient GinkgoTree Planted 1,000 years ago during the Liao Dynasty, the tree is a tourist attraction of the temple.

辽代石碑　为寺中六绝之一，碑上“晹台山清水院藏经记”字样依稀可辨。

Liao Dynasty Stele The stele was made during the 10th century. The characters inscribed on the stone “A note about the construction and scripture keeping of the Qingshuiyuan Temple on Yangtai Mountain” are still visible.

龙潭　潭水由山泉汇集而成，水清甘冽，为寺中六绝之一。

Dragon Pool　The pool collects cool and clear water from mountain springs.

妙应寺
THE MIAOYING TEMPLE

北京城有两座著名的藏式白塔，相距不及10公里，东西相望，东为永安寺白塔，西为妙应寺白塔。两塔的知名度远在其寺之上。

妙应寺白塔先于寺而建。辽代曾在燕京城的五方建五色塔，不久皆先后倾颓。公元1271年，元世祖忽必烈敕令在白塔旧基上重建新塔，工程由尼泊尔杰出匠师阿尼哥主持，于1279年竣工。塔成之后，忽必烈命人以塔为中心，向四面各射一箭，以箭落处为界划定寺址，面积约16万平方米，赐名大圣寿万安寺。十三、四世纪时，该寺曾是元皇室在京城举行宗教活动和译经的场所。

公元1368年寺遭焚，公元1457年重建，改名妙应寺。重建时，殿宇皆改置于塔前。主要建筑有山门、钟鼓楼、天王殿、意珠心镜殿、七佛宝殿，面积只及原来的十二分之一。今日妙应寺除山门、钟鼓楼被拆除外，其余均保持重建后的格局。

There are two famous white pagodas in Tibetan style in Beijing, one in the Yong'an Temple in the east and the other in the Miaoying Temple in the west. Ten kilometers apart, they are much more famous than the temples where they are located. The pagoda in the Miaoying Temple was built before the temple. The rulers of the Liao Dynasty built five pagodas of five colors in five directions in Beijing. But they collapsed not long afterwards. Kublai Khan of the Yuan Dynasty ordered a Nepal architect to rebuild the white one on the original site. When the reconstruction was completed in 1279 Kublai Khan shot four arrows in four directions and ordered a temple be built within the border where the arrows reached. He named it Dashengshou Wan'an Temple. The gigantic project on 160,000 square meters was carried on over half a century. In the 13th and 14th centuries, the temple served as the spot of imperial court service and Buddhist scripture translation.

The temple was burnt down in 1368 and rebuilt in 1457. Its name changed to Miaoying. During the reconstruction, all the halls were moved before the pagoda. Main structures are the front gate, drum and bell towers, Heavenly King Hall, the Hall of Yizhu Xinjing and the Hall of Seven Buddhas. The scale was reduced by 12 times. The temple today has retained the outlook of the reconstruction except that the front gate and drum and bell towers had been removed.

三世佛 供于七佛宝殿，元代遗存，用楠木雕琢而成，各高 3.3 米。中为释迦牟尼及其弟子迦叶和阿难，其左右是东方净琉璃世界的药师佛和西方极乐世界的阿弥陀佛。

Trikala Buddhas The nanmu wood statues of Trikala Buddhas in the Hall of Seven Buddhas were carved during the Yuan Dynasty, each 3.3 meters high. In the middle are Sakyamuni and his disciples Kasyapa and Ananda. On the left is Bhaisajyagura of the East Land and Amitabha of the East Joyful Land.

七佛宝殿藻井 殿顶上共有三个形状、大小、纹饰相同的藻井，上雕九龙十二凤，寓意“龙凤呈祥”。

Caisson of the Hall of Seven Buddhas On the ceiling of the hall there are three caissons of the same shape, size and decoration. They are carved with nine dragons and 12 phoenixes.

千眼千手观音 铜质，高2米，清代铸造。此像供于七佛宝殿，三世佛屏后，其造型奇异，共有十一面，即佛头四面，冠上底层四面，中层两面，顶层一面，所以又称十一面观音。

Avalokitesvara of 1,000 Eyes and 1,000 Hands The copper statue of two meters high was cast during the Qing Dynasty. It is worshipped behind the statues of Trikala Buddhas in the Hall of Seven Buddhas. The statue has 11 sides: the head has four sides, the bottom of the crown has four sides, the middle part of the crown has two sides and the top of the crown has one side. The unique statue is also called the 11-side Avalokitesvara.

护法神像 立于七佛宝殿两侧，共十八尊，明代铸造，铜质鎏金。此为其中之一摩利支天。

Statues of Law Guardians The 18 gilt copper Law Guardians stand on the two sides in the Hall of Seven Buddhas. They were made during the Ming Dynasty. This is one of them.

妙应寺白塔 塔高 51 米，底座面积 1422 平方米，其势巍峨宏丽，数公里外可见其雄姿。

The Miaoying Temple The white pagoda behind the temple is 51 meters high and stands on a 810-square-meter base. It can be seen several kilometers away.

镇寺宝物 白塔建成后七百年间，曾经过十次较大的修缮，1978 年整修时，在塔顶发现一批佛教文物，为公元 1753 年修葺后放置的镇寺之宝。图为其中两件:

The white pagoda has undertaken ten major repairs during the 700 years since its construction. In the repair in 1978 some cultural relics were discovered. They were confirmed as being stored in it in 1753. These are two objects:

五佛冠 此冠镶有珍珠、珊瑚珠、檀木珠和宝石千余颗，十分珍贵。

2. **The Crown of Five Buddhas** It is inlaid with more than 1,000 pieces of pearls, coral beads, sandlewood beads and precious stones.

赤金舍利长寿佛 高约 5 厘米，上嵌 44 颗红宝石和一粒舍利子。

1. **Gold Sariputra** The five-centimeter-high statue is inlaid with 44 pieces of ruby and a crystalized bit of Sakyamuni's ashes.

国子监牌楼 孔庙所在的成贤街两端各建有一座牌楼，这条街僻静安谧，古貌依存。

Archways of Guozijian At either end of Chengxian Street where Confucius Temple is located there is an archway, enhancing the tranquility and archaic atmosphere of the street.

孔 庙
CONFUCIUS TEMPLE

孔庙是祭祀中国古代思想家孔子的庙宇。孔子名丘（公元前 551–前 479 年），字仲尼，是春秋时期（公元前 770–前 476 年）人。他创立的儒家学派主张德治、仁政，崇尚伦理道德，得到了历代封建君主的推崇，尊之为先师、先贤、先圣，并在各地建庙祭祀。

北京孔庙建成于公元 1306 年，规模仅次于孔子故里山东曲阜的孔庙，为中国第二大孔庙。它位于城区东北安定门内成贤街（又名国子监街）北侧。庙占地面积约 2.2 万平方米，以大成殿为中心，前有先师门、大成门，后有供奉孔子先祖牌位的崇圣祠。大成门外有神厨、井亭、宰牲亭、致斋所、神库等。庙内尚有碑亭 14 座，碑林两处。

Confucius (Kong Qiu, also known as Zhongni) lived between 551-479 B.C. during the Spring and Autunm Period (770-476 B.C.). Confunicianism founded by him advocates the rule of virtue and benevolence and stresses good morals. Rulers through the Chinese history all promoted his principles, confered on him honorary titles such as "the late teacher", "the late sage" and "the late great man", and built temples in his honor.

The Confucius Temple in Beijing was built in 1306, only smaller than that in Confucius' birthplace, Qufu in Shandong Province. It is located on Chengxian Street (also called Guozijian) in northeastern part of the city and covers 22,000 square meters. Before the main Dacheng Hall are the Late Teacher's Gate and Dacheng Gate, behind the hall is Congsheng Shrine in which tablets of Confucius' ancestors are worshipped. Outside the Dacheng Gate there are the Divine Kitchen, Well Pavilion, Sacrificial Pavilion, Fast Room and Divine Store. The temple also has 14 stele pavilions and two groups of stone tablets.

先师门 为孔庙大门，面阔三间，虽经历代修葺，仍保留了原建规制，其斗拱硕大稀疏，展示了元代浑厚、古朴、简洁的建筑风格。

The Late Teacher's Gate The front gate of Confucius Temple has retained the original style though it has undertaken repairs on many occasions. The huge brackets sparsely arranged show the simple and round style of ancient times.

大成门　古谓孔子思想集中国古文化之大成，所以庙中殿、门皆以“大成”名之。

The Dacheng Gate　Dacheng in Chinese means the collection of all the good things. Confucianism is the collection of all the good things of ancient culture of China. So many places related to Confucius are called Dacheng.

石雕　镶嵌于大成殿前，整块汉白玉石上雕刻着云、龙图案，刻工精细，堪为浮雕珍品。

Stone Carvings Ona whole piece of white marble in front of the Dacheng Hall are carved in relief designs of clouds and dragons with high craftsmanship.

大成殿侧视　大成殿为孔庙正殿，面宽九间深五进，双层飞檐，红壁，黄琉璃瓦覆顶，高耸于汉白玉月台之上，俨然为皇家宫殿规制。殿前古柏已有 600 多年历史，据民间传说，明代奸相严嵩代嘉靖皇帝来此祭孔，被柏枝掀掉了乌纱帽，严被罢相后，人们称此柏为“除奸柏”。

A Side View of the Dacheng Hall
The Dacheng Hall, the main hall of the Confucius Temple, has double, flying eaves, crimson walls and yellow glazed-tile roof. It stands majesticaly on a white marble terrace in immitation of imperial palaces. The cypress trees in front of it are more than 500 years old. A folk tale tells that when Yan Song, the sinister prime minister, came on behalf of Emperor Jia Qing of the Ming Dynasty to pay respect to Confucius his hat was brushed off his head by a branch of a cypress tree. After Yan Song was dismissed from the office people named the tree “Tree Expelling the Evil”.

大成殿内景 正中设木龛，龛内置孔子木牌位，上书历代帝王加封的谥号“大成至圣文宣王”。

Inside the Dacheng Hall In a wooden niche in the middle of the Dacheng Hall is a wooden tablet bearing the title bestowed on Confucius by imperial rulers: “The King of Dacheng Zhisheng Wenxuan”.

祭孔盛典 历史上一年三祭的仪典分别于农历二月和八月上旬的丁日及孔子诞辰日举行。届时，由皇帝主祭，仪程有奏乐、迎神、跳八佾舞、跪拜、送神等。

Ceremony to Honor Confucius The ceremony to honor Confucius took place on three occasions: in the second month and eighth month of the lunar callendar and on the birthday of Confucius. A tribute was read by the emperor. The whole process was composed of music playing, receiving the gods, Bayi dance, kowtowing to Confucius and sending off the gods.

碑林 孔庙内珍存历代石碑 400 余座，其中有进士题名碑 198 座、记功记事碑 14 座、十三经刻石碑 189 座。图为十三经刻石碑林，是中国目前最完整的十三经刻石，因刻于清乾隆年间，所以又称“乾隆石经”。

Stele Forest The Confucius Temple keeps more than 400 stone tablets, 198 of which bear the names of successful candidates of imperial examinations, 14 of which record meritorious deeds and events, 190 of which bear inscriptions of 13 classical writings and two of which are inscriptions on stone drums. The picture shows stone tablets bear inscriptions of 13 classical writings. Because they were carved during the reign of Emperor Qian Long, they are also known as “Stone Classics of Qian Long”.

碧 云 寺
THE BIYUN TEMPLE

寺座落在香山东麓，是一座构筑精丽的古刹，古人说它"金碧鲜妍，宛一天界"。

据碑文记载，寺前身是元代官家私宅，公元 1289 年改宅为庙，名碧云庵。公元 1516 年和 1623 年明代太监于经、魏忠贤先后扩建，并易名为于公寺和碧云寺。于、魏二人都是当朝宠臣，扩建时不惜财力，极尽华美。

寺的中部有五座殿堂，由山麓至山巅层层迭起，高低相差百余米。各层殿庭毗连相通，又自成格局，曲折多致。

寺后最高处是公元 1748 年建造的金刚宝座塔。寺南侧有与塔同年所建的罗汉堂，寺北侧建有以山泉和池桥取胜的水泉院、碧涵斋。

远眺碧云寺 在如画的北京西山群峰间，碧云寺独居一峰。寺后的石塔与玉泉山玉峰塔遥遥相对，构成一幅如诗如画的美景。

The Biyun Temple seen from afar
The Biyuan Temple occupies a peak among the peaks of the West Mountains in Beijing. A stone pagoda behind the temple and the pagoda on the Jade Spring Hill make up a beautiful picture.

The Biyun Temple is located on the eastern side of Xiangshan (Fragrant Hill) in the western suburbs of Beijing. It used to be a private residence of a court official during the Yuan Dynasty and was converted into a Buddhist temple in 1366. It was enlarged in 1516 and 1623 by eunuchs Yu Jing and Wei Zhongxian of the Ming Dynasty. The two powerful eunuchs spent exubitant amount of money and manpower to make the temple as majestic as possible.

The five halls rise tier upon tier on a slope, each within a drop of 100 meters. They are independent yet connected by flights of steps or zigzag paths. The diamond-seat with five pagodas on the very top was built in 1748. A hall with 500 arhats in the western part of the temple was also built in that year. The Foundain Compound and Bihan Studio in the eastern part of the temple are famous for a mountain spring, pond and bridge.

碧云寺山门 山门前是一座架于两峭壁上的石桥，四周古木参天，绿荫浓郁；桥下是深约 15 米的涧壑，有山泉从寺内流出，直泻涧底，形成一股四季不竭的小瀑布，造就了碧云寺第一景。图为夜景。

The front gate of the Biyun Temple
In front of the gate is a stone bridge spanning two sheer cliffs. Around it are ancient trees. The gully under the bridge is 15 meters deep. Mountain spring water flows from inside the temple into the gully. This is a night scene at the bridge.

弥勒佛　供奉于天王殿正中，铸于明代，铜质，高2.5米。此佛笑容满面，仪态慈祥可亲。相传他是十世纪初的一名游方僧，名契此，号长汀子，在世时常持一布袋行乞，所得钱物悉数捐赠寺院，所以人们又称他为“布袋僧”。

Maitreya Buddha　The 2.5-meter-high copper statue in the Heavenly King Hall was made during the Ming Dynasty. A story tells that he was a migrant Buddhist monk named Qibi, also known as Changdingzi and collected alms with a cloth bag. He donated what he collected to temples. So people also call him Cloth Bag Monk.

丹青阁 为寺之主殿，系明代建筑，面阔五间，方形庑殿式殿顶。殿前立一对高约 8 米的六角形汉白玉石经幢。殿内正位供释迦牟尼坐像，姿态似讲经说法。殿壁上有唐玄奘西天取经故事的雕塑，刻划细腻，人物形象生动逼真。

Danqing Tower The main structure in the temple was built during the Ming Dynasty in the style of imperial palaces. In front of the tower there are two eight-meter-high stone pillars inscribed with Buddhist scriptures, and inside it is a seated statue of Sakyamuni as if preaching. On the wall are carvings in relief depicting Monk Xuan Zang of the Tang Dynasty traveling to the west to fetch scriptures.

水泉院 原为乾隆皇帝行宫的一部分，院内松柏参天，层层叠石，清泉汀淙，亭台小桥点缀其间，颇具江南风光。

The Foundain Compound It was once a part of a temporary palace of Emperor Qian Long. In the compound there are ancient pine and cypress trees, a pool of foundain water, pavilion and bridge, an exquisite scene usually found south of the Yangtze River.

石坊　位于金刚宝座塔正面，坊长34米，高约10米，汉白玉石结构，牌坊上布满精美浮雕，它是北京寺庙中颇具特色的一座牌坊。

Stone Archway　The archway of white marble in front of the Diamond Seat with pagodas is 34 meters long and 10 meters high. Carvings in relief on the archway are of high craftsmanship. It is a unique archway of its kind in the Beijing area.

金刚宝座塔　为全寺最高建筑物，塔座呈正方形，整塔高 34.7 米。此塔在造型上吸收了印度佛陀迦耶精舍的形式，但在建筑手法和雕刻艺术上却突出地表现了中国传统的建筑风格。

The Diamond Seat with Pagodas

The 34.7-meter-high square structure occupies the highest point of the temple. It looks much like the Gaya Temple of India but the architecture and carvings are conspicuously Chinese.

罗汉堂 其平面呈“田”字形，堂内有500尊罗汉，7尊神像，还有蹲在梁上的济公，共508尊。据佛教故事说，释迦牟尼圆寂后，其弟子们四次聚会，会诵、审定以往口述的佛经。五百罗汉就是曾参加过聚会的五百比丘。

The Arhat Hall The hall houses 500 arhats, seven gods and Master Jigong squatting on a rafter, making it 508 statues in all. According to Buddhism, after Sakyamuni's death his disciples gathered together to pray and examine the oral teachings of Sakyamuni. They are the 500 arhats now worshipped in this hall.

罗汉 五百罗汉各高1.5米，均为木胎泥塑，外部饰金，神情仪态各不相同，是清代雕塑艺术中的佳品。

Arhats The 1.5-meter-high statues are made with clay on wooden frames and guilted. They are the cream of sculptures of the Qing Dynasty.

广化寺
THE GUANGHUA TEMPLE

北京城区西北地安门外，有一狭长形湖泊，名叫什刹海，它北连积水潭，南与紫禁城西面的中海、南海、北海相通。这里垂柳绕岸，莲荷田田。明清以来，许多皇亲国戚竞相在湖畔建府造园，修筑寺庙。广化寺即建于湖的东岸。

广化寺始建于元代，十六世纪和十九世纪中叶曾两次重修。公元1894年再次重建，现在基本保持重建后的格局。全寺建筑共分五路，除一般寺庙的中、东、西路以外，又在两旁增建东二路和西二路，因而更显得宏阔严整。

寺内仍保留佛像、佛坛和多种古版《大藏经》、《大日本续藏经》等佛经珍本。

北京市佛教协会设于寺内。

The temple is located on the eastern bank of Shishahai Lake in the northwestern part of Beijing city. Shishahai is connected with Jishuitan Lake to its north and Zhonghai, Nanhai and Beihai lakes to its south. The Forbidden City is on the west shore of the three lakes. In old days the shore was decorated with willow trees and lotus ponds. During the Ming and Qing dynasties many members of the royal family and high-ranking officials built mansions, gardens and temples on the shore. Among the major temples is the Guanghua.

The Guanghua Temple was built during the Yuan Dynasty and was renovated twice during the 16th and mid-19th centuries. A reconstruction was carried out in 1894. The present temple has retained the scale of that time. Usually a Buddhist temple is made up with structures on three lines. The Guanghua has five lines of buildings, making it more magnificent.

The temple keeps Buddha statues, Buddha niches and rare copies of Buddhist scriptures including the Collection of Scriptures and Extended Collection of Scriptures

The temple houses the Beijing Assocation of Buddhism.

古朴庄重的山门 The front gate

殿中的观音立像
Standing statue of Avalokitesvara

大雄宝殿　面广五间，重檐歇山式殿顶，轩敞宏阔。

The Daxiong Hall　It is five-bay wide and has a gabled roof.

金刚宝座塔　是中国现存同样形式中较为古老、精美的一座宝塔。其造型源于印度佛陀迦耶精舍，即在金刚宝座上建造 5 座小塔。塔用砖砌成，外表用青白石贴面，并在宝座四周、小塔基座和塔檐之间遍凿精美的佛教雕刻。雕刻手法圆润流畅，是不可多得的明代巨大石雕艺术品。

Five pagodas on the Diamond Seat
The style of five pagodas on one base follows the style of the Gaya Temple of India. The pagodas are built with bricks and lined with bluish stoneslabs. Buddhist carvings are seen on the four walls of the main base and the bases of the pagodas. Those in the Zhenjue Temple are highly valued for their superb craftsmanship from the Ming Dynasty.

真 觉 寺
THE ZHENJUE TEMPLE

位于北京西直门外，古柳夹岸的长河自西北东流入城。十五至十九世纪时，长河沿岸寺庙相望，钟鼓相闻，善男信女不绝于道，是京城近郊的朝佛游胜之地。

真觉寺创建于明永乐年间（公元1403–1424年），公元1761年曾改名大正觉寺，由于寺中有集五塔为一体的金刚宝座塔，所以人们皆称它五塔寺。

寺内殿宇早已无存，所存主要建筑唯有建于公元1473年的金刚宝座塔。这种形式的塔中国目前仅存近十座，北京共四座即真觉寺塔、碧云寺塔、西黄寺塔以及妙高塔，而以真觉寺塔建造年代最早。

寺内辟有石刻艺术博物馆，共陈列各类石刻文物1200余件，可谓北京石刻大观。

The temple outside the Xizhimen city gate stands on the Changhe River which flows into Beijing city from northwest to east. During the 15th and 19th centuries there were many Buddhist temples along the river. The sound of drums and bells were heard continuously, and pilgrams were numerous. Now only the Zhenjue and Wanshou temples exist.

The Zhenjue Temple was built between 1403 and 1424 during the Ming Dynasty. In 1761 its name changed to Dazhengjue. There are five pagodas on one base. So the temple is popularly known as Five Pagoda Temple.

All the halls have long gone. Only the base with five pagodas built in 1473 stands on the old site. In China there are ten groups of five pagodas, and four are in Beijing in the Zhenjue Temple, Biyun Temple, West Huang Temple and the Miaogao Pagodas. The group in the Zhenjue Temple is the oldest.

The Stone Sculpture Museum in the temple has on display 1,200 stone carvings from ancient times.

鸟瞰真觉寺
A bird's-eye view of the Zhenjue Temple.

五塔之一 五座塔均为方形密檐式，居中的一座大塔，共13层，高约8米；四角小塔各11层，高约7米。图为小塔之一。

One of the five pagodas The five pagodas have square roofs of several layers. The largest one in the middle is 13 meters high of 13 tiers. The four smaller pagodas are seven meters high of 11 tiers. The picture shows one of the smaller pagodas.

佛足 刻于中塔基座，如真人足掌大小。相传是释迦牟尼圆寂时伸出灵床外的双足。佛教徒膜拜时，以头顶足印，表示对佛的敬仰。

The feet of the Buddha The Buddha's feet carved on the base of the middle pagoda are the same size of a real person. It is said they were the feet of Sakyamuni on his deathbed. Buddhists pay their respect to the Buddha by touching their heads against the feet.

金刚宝座雕刻 采用的是古朴的"减地平级"法，即凸起的主题雕刻面与凹进的"地"都是平的，然后用尖刀在突起的主题面上刻出细而流畅的线条，使得主体形象突出并有立体感。雕刻内容多是密宗题材，以佛像为主，共 1561 尊；其次是狮、象、马、孔雀及大鹏金翅鸟。整个雕刻动中有静，静中有动，妙趣横生，使人叹为观止。

Carvings on the main base The carvings in relief are unique because all the incave and concave areas are flat. Flowy lines were made by sharp knives on the concave areas. Most of the pictures depict stories of the Mi sect of Buddhism, with 1,561 Buddhas as the main theme. Other topics are lions, elephants, horses, peacocks and rocs.

碑林一角　寺内收藏各种石碑、碑刻千余件，图为龙顶龟趺竖碑。

Part of the Stele Forest　The temple keeps more than 1,000 pieces of stone with inscriptions. The picture shows a vertical stele standing on a turtle with a dragon crown.

卧碑 此碑为普胜寺卧碑，立于清顺治八年（公元 1651 年），其形制为大型卧式，异于常见的竖碑。

Horizontal Stele The stone tablet used to be kept in the Pusheng Temple. It was built in 1651 during the Ming Dynasty. It is rare because most stone tablets are in vertical position.

法海寺全景 寺座落在翠微山南麓，这里松柏葱茏，满目青翠。

The Fahai Temple The temple on Cuiwei Mountain is surrounded by luxuriant pine and crypress trees.

法 海 寺
THE FAHAI TEMPLE

位于西郊石景山区翠微山南麓，寺因存有绘制精湛的佛教壁画而闻名。

寺由明代太监李童集资兴建，公元 1439 年动工，历时四年殿宇与壁画同时完成。寺内原有天王殿、伽蓝殿、护法金刚殿、大雄宝殿、祖师堂、钟鼓楼等。由于年久失修，除绘有壁画的大雄宝殿外，皆已倾圮，近年来正陆续重建。

壁画面积共 236.7 平方米，绘于大雄宝殿内壁。殿中扇面墙两侧、东西山墙和后檐墙分别绘诸天礼佛图、五方佛胜境图和飞天，扇面墙背面绘有水月观音、文殊、普贤三菩萨。共绘佛、菩萨、天神、仙女等 70 余众，刻画得精细入微，富有变化。壁画采用中国传统的工笔重彩法和多种用金的技法，因此，色彩明艳，富丽堂皇，被有关专家誉之为中国明代壁画之最。虽然历经五个多世纪，画面依然清晰完好。从寺中经幢上得知，壁画皆出自明代宫廷画师之手。

The temple on the southern side of Cuiwei Mountain in Shijingshan District on the western outskirts of Beijing is famous for Buddhist murals. It was built with funds collected by eunuch Li Tong of the Ming Dynasty. Construction began in 1439 and was completed in four years. Because of neglect of many years, the original Heavenly King Hall, Sangharama Hall, Dvarapala Hall, Masters' Hall and bell and drum towers had collapsed long ago. Only the Daxiong Hall with murals has remained. In recent years a reconstruction has been carried out.

The murals in the Daxiong Hall cover 236.7 square meters. They depict the worship of Buddha, holy lands in five directions, flying Apsaras, Bodhisattva Buddhas of Water and Moon, Wisdom and Universal Benevolence. The more than 70 images of Buddhas, heavenly deities and fairies are meticulously painted with Chinese traditional techniques. The colors are bright. A note inscribed on a stone pillar tells that the murals were painted by court painters of the Ming Dynasty. Specialists believe they are the best murals from that time.

大雄宝殿 位于寺院北端。殿前两株白皮松相传为建寺之初所植，至今枝叶茂盛，荫覆半院。

The Daxiong Hall It is located at the northern tip of the temple. Two lacebark pine trees in front of it were planted at the time of the temple's construction and are still flourishing.

广目天王 北壁西侧壁画，此神形貌威猛，须发、衣纹、佩饰描绘得精细入微。

Western Lockapala The god is one of the four Heavenly Kings. His hair and beard, clothes and ornaments are meticulously painted.

飞天 山墙西侧壁画，其线条流畅潇洒，富有表现力，所绘祥云、衣裙飘逸洒脱，给人以古朴缥渺之感。

Flying apsaras The heavenly figures painted on the wall have fluent lines and vivid expressions in an archaic style.

帝释梵天图（局部） 北壁东侧壁画，全图分绘于北门两侧，表现诸天神众礼佛护法的场景，共绘 30 余人，依序排列，顾盼呼应。人物动静不一，各有情致：帝后文静慈祥，武将英气勃发，神怪则面目狰狞。

Worshipping the Buddha (detail) The pictures on the eastern part of the northern wall show the scene of more than 30 gods and the king and empress worshipping the Buddha.

智 化 寺
THE ZHIHUA TEMPLE

位于东城区一条民居稠密的古老街巷——禄米仓胡同东口。

智化寺始建于公元1443年，原是明代司礼监太监王振自建的家庙。寺建成方六年，王振在宫廷之争中被诛，寺被充作公产。

寺虽为家庙，但建筑格局却严守中国古寺规制。全寺分三路，中路分前、中、后三院，前院共有七座殿堂，中院仅建一如来殿，后院建有大悲堂、万佛堂。山门两侧有东、西旁门，入门后沿着长长的甬道，西可抵方丈院，东可至后庙。

寺内藏有十八世纪镌刻的大藏经版，是中国现今仅存的一套官刻汉文佛教经版，因是皇帝下令镌刻的，所以尊之为《龙藏经》。

The Zhihua Temple is located at the eastern entrance to Lumicang Lane, an ancient side street in eastern part of Beijing. Eunuch Wang Zhen of the Ming Dynasty built it in 1443 as his family shrine. Six years later the eunuch was executed and the temple was confiscated by the imperial court. Although it was originally a family shrine, the temple is strictly laid out according to the rules of official Buddhist temples. It is composed of three compounds. There are seven halls in the front compound. The compound in the middle has the Tathagata Buddha Hall and the rear compound has the Dabei Hall and 10,000-Buddha Hall. Long corridors from the two side gates lead to the abot's quarter and rear halls.

The temple keeps the wood blocks for printing the "Grand Collection of Buddhist Scriptures". Made during the Ming Dynasty by an imperial decree, they are the only officially carved blocks in Chinese language. Because they were made by an imperial decree, they are respectfully called the "Dragon Scriptures"

三身佛像 供奉于万佛阁，三身佛即法身佛毗卢遮那佛，报身佛卢舍那佛和应身佛释迦牟尼佛。佛教教理说，释迦牟尼以此三身传法。

The Three Bodies of Buddha The three bodies of the Buddha in the 10,000-Buddhas Hall are Vairocana, Sambhoga-kaya and Sakyamuni. They represent the law body, spiritual body and physical body of Sakyamuni.

《龙藏经》经版 经版选用上等梨木雕成，共有 78，230 块，从清雍正十二年（1733 年）至乾隆三年（1738 年）刊刻了 6 年才完成，刻成后 300 多年间，流行的印本不过 200 部。经版至今完整如新。

Blocks of the "Dragon Scriptures" The 78,230 blocks are of high quality pear wood. Carving began in 1733 and was finished in 1738. During the 300 years after the blocks were carved, 200 editions have been printed with them.

如来殿万佛阁 为寺内中院的主要建筑，此殿面阔三间，为重檐歇山顶，分上下两层，下层供如来佛楠木雕像，高约 3 米，故称如来殿；因楼内上下壁遍饰佛龛，每龛内供高约 13 厘米的佛像，总数约万尊，所以上层额书万佛阁。

The 10,000-Buddha Tower and Tathagata Buddha Hall The two-in-in main structure in the temple is of two stories with a gabled roof. The upper floor has a nanmu wood statue of Tathagata Buddha of three meters high. About 10,000 Buddhist statues of 13 centimeters high are placed in the many niches in the hall.

广 济 寺
THE GUANGJI TEMPLE

为北京著名佛教古寺之一，创建于金代。

相传十二世纪时北京西四一带尚为郊野，村民曾在此自建一座乡间寺院，名西刘村寺。十五世纪寺圮废，人们在掘地时发现了陶制佛像、供器、石龟、石柱顶等物，始知此处为古刹遗址。明天顺年间（公元 1457–1464 年）僧人普慧及其弟子圆洪募资重建，得到明皇室支持，并赐名弘慈广济寺。

寺内主要建筑有山门、天王殿、大雄殿、圆通殿、多宝殿、藏经阁，以及十七世纪末增筑的戒坛。

寺中藏有珍贵的经卷 10 余万册，内有全套明版大藏经；还有房山云居寺石经拓片 3 万余片，云居寺出土的静琬法师舍利子，以及诸多碑刻和佛教文物等，堪称一座佛教博物馆。

中国佛教协会和中国佛学研究所均设于寺内。

韦驮菩萨铜像　铸于明代。韦驮是佛教护法神，一说是四大天王属下的三十二神将之首，所以各寺庙常置于前殿，背主佛而立，充任守卫。

Copper statue of Skanda It was cast in the Ming Dynasty. Skanda is a guardian deity of law, the first of the 32 generals under the four Heavenly Kings. Usually the statue of Skanda stands with his back to the Buddha in the front hall of a temple.

The Buddhist temple was built during the Jin Dynasty (1115-1234).

During the 12th century the area around Xisi in the Beijing city was still vacant ground. Villagers built a temple and named it Liu Village Temple. It was abandoned in the 15th century and soon forgotten. Later pottery Buddhist statues, sacrificial objects, stone turtles and pillars were unearthed from the site. Between 1457 and 1464 Buddhist monk Pu Hui and his disciple Yuan Hong collected funds and rebuilt the temple and named it Hongci Guangji. The Ming imperial court also gave some money.

Main structures of the temple are the front gate, Heavenly King Hall, Daxiong Hall, Yuantong Hall, Duobao Hall, Scripture Tower and an ordination terrace built in the 17th century. The temple keeps more than 100,000 copies of rare scriptures including a complete set of the "Grand Collection of Scriptures" printed during the Ming Dynasty, 30,000 stone slabs with scriptures from the Yunju Temple, granulated ashes of Monk Jing Wan unearthed from the Yunju Temple, and many stone inscriptions and Buddhist relics.

The temple houses the office of the China Buddhist Association and China Buddhism Research Institute.

山门　山门有券门三座，正中的券门上方嵌有"敕建弘慈广济寺"石额，为清康熙皇帝御书。

The front gate The name plaque above the middle entrance of the front gate is in the handwriting of Emperor Kang Xi of the Qing Dynasty.

大雄殿殿脊 俗称香水海，又名华藏世界海，整体呈山形，由水、莲花和一个梵文字构成，字的含意是，永恒世界，不生不灭。此种殿脊，在北京地区独此一家。

Roof ridge of the Daxiong Hall Commonly called Fragrant Water Sea or World Sea, the ridge in the form of a hill has designs of water, lotus flowers and a Sanskrit letter meaning everlasting world. The Guuangji Temple is the only Buddhist temple in Beijing to have such a roof ridge.

大雄殿 殿前立有明清石碑四座，庭中置清代所铸八宝纹青铜鼎。

The Daxiong Hall The four stone tablets in front of the hall were made during the Ming and Qing dynasties. A bronze pot made during the Qing Dynasty is placed inside the hall.

弥勒铜佛 供于天王殿，明代铸造。像身着佛装，面容慈善，仪态安详，与别寺所供的大肚弥勒形象相去甚远。

Copper statue of Maitreya Buddha The statue in the Heavenly King Hall was cast during the Ming Dynasty. The Buddha has a kind and dignified expression, very different from other statues of Miatreya Buddha that invariably have a huge belly and broad smile.

大雄殿内景　内供三世佛像，中为释迦牟尼佛，其右为燃灯佛，其左为弥勒佛。

Inside the Daxiong Hall　Of the Trikala Buddhas the middle one is Sakyamuni. On his right is Dipamkara Buddha and on his left is Maitreya Buddha.

十八罗汉 供于大雄殿东西两侧，在北京寺庙中，铜铸十八罗汉并置于佛龛内，实不多见。图为右侧九尊罗汉。

18 Arhats They stand on the eastern and western sides in the Daxiong Hall. It is rare in Beijing to put copper statues of 18 arhats in niches. The picture shows the nine arhats on the right side.

大慧寺
THE DAHUI TEMPLE

位于西直门外大柳树北村，南距真觉寺约1公里。

寺始建于公元1513年，现寺中建筑仅余一大悲殿。殿内原供有高16米余的大铜佛，故寺曾名大佛寺。大佛于本世纪四十年代被侵华日军所毁，所幸殿内的佛教雕像和壁画尚完好无损。

殿内共有二十八尊诸天护法神像，为十六世纪明代的作品。像为夹纻彩塑，均高3米，立于须弥座上，几乎齐及殿顶，奇伟异常。诸神塑得形象丰满，精微传神。

大殿内壁绘有彩色工笔连环画，描绘一人终生行善，感动了神佛，最后超度成仙。壁画从侧面反映了明代的社会生活和民间习尚。

劫后独存的大悲殿集明代建筑、雕塑、壁画于一体，实为北京今存的佛教艺术中的绝品。

The Dahui Temple at the North Daliushu Village outside the Xizhimen city gate is one kilometer north of the Zhenjue Temple. It was built in 1513 and called Giant Buddha Temple because there used to be a copper statue of Buddha more than 16 meters high. The statue was destroyed by the Japanese invaders in the 1940s. All the halls but the Dabei Hall were long gone. Some Buddhist statues and murals have remained in the Dabei Hall.

The 28 statues of Divine Guardians of Law of clay with hemp inforcement were made during the Ming Dynasty. Three meters high, they stand on Sumeru seats and reach almost to the ceiling. Pictures on the walls inside the hall depict a man who did good deeds all his life and the Buddha was moved to make him immortal. The pictures reflect the daily life and customs of the people during the Ming Dynasty.

The architecture of the Dabei Hall and sculptures and wall paintings in it are treasures of Buddhist art.

壁画局部 壁画采用中国传统的通景式构图法，将众多的故事绘于连续而又独立的画面中。

Details of murals The murals in the Dabei Hall were painted in Chinese traditional style — all scenes are depicted in one single space but each can be reviewed as an independent part.

大悲殿 面宽五间，进深三间，重檐庑殿顶，仍保留明代建筑法式。

The Dabei Hall The palatial structure of several eaves is typical of the Ming Dynasty architectural style.

天王塑像　人物造型威武剽悍，衣饰褶纹叠皱，几可以假乱真。

Statues of Heavenly Kings　The gods look very militant; and the clothes seem to be real.

护法神　其衣边上的描金纹饰，至今仍金色灿然。

Divine Guardians of Law　The gold paint on the reams of the clothes of the gods is still shining after several hundred years.

殿内彩塑神像　诸神的神情、体态、面貌都依其身份而异，是世间各类人物的写照。

Colored statues in the hall　The expressions and physical postures of the gods vary from one to another according to their positions, representing people of all walks of life.

慈寿寺
THE CISHOU TEMPLE

位于阜成门外八里庄，距城约 4 公里。

寺建于明万历四年（公元 1576 年），是明代万历皇帝的生母李太后所建。万历皇帝即位时年仅十岁，内外政事一度由李太后执掌。太后平生好佛，在她主政期间命人在京城内外兴建、修缮了多座佛寺，慈寿寺即是那一时期建造的。

寺中殿宇已废弃近百年，寺址上仅余一塔，塔原名永安万寿塔，据说是仿天宁寺塔而建，但是建筑手法和雕饰艺术仍具有明代风格。塔高 50 米，共十三层，为八角形密檐式实心砖塔，造型挺拔秀美。塔的基座、塔身和塔檐上的雕饰精细而逼真。虽历经数百年依然清晰可见。是北京现存明塔的代表作。

The Cishou Temple is located at Balizhuang outside the Fuchengmen city gate, four kilometers west of the city proper. It was built in 1576 by Emperor Wan Li of the Ming Dynasty for his mother, EmpressDowager Li. The emperor ascended the throne at the age of 10. All the state affairs were handled by his mother. Empress Dowager Li was a devoted Buddhist and built several Buddhist temples in Beijing. The Cishou was one of them.

All the halls in the temple were long gone. Only a pagoda has been left named Yong'an Wanshou. It is said the pagoda was an imitation of the pagoda of the Tianning Temple. The architecture and carving are typical the Ming Dynasty style. The octagonal pagoda of solid bricks are 50 meters high and of 13 tiers. The carvings on the base, body and eaves are elaborate and life like. The pagoda is a representative of Ming pagodas in the Beijing area.

第一层塔身上的雕饰

Carvings on the first tier of the pagoda.

慈寿寺塔

The Pàgoda of the Cishou Temple.

层层相叠的塔檐细部

Details of the closely arranged eaves.

万 寿 寺
THE WANSHOU TEMPLE

由真觉寺沿长河西行1公里余，便可抵达濒临长河北岸的万寿寺。

寺建成于公元1578年，是明万历皇帝之母李太后继慈寿寺后兴建的又一座佛刹。公元1751年和1761年，清乾隆皇帝为了给其母祝寿，曾两次修缮、扩建万寿寺，使其成为一座集寺庙、园林、行宫为一体的皇家名刹。

全寺建筑分三路。中路由南至北依次为山门、天王殿、大雄宝殿、万寿阁、大禅堂、大士殿、无量寿佛殿。东路为方丈院。西路是行宫院，院内房舍装修华丽，宛若御苑。

清代帝后由水路至颐和园和西山游幸，行至万寿寺以东的广源闸时，要登岸换船，必入寺烧香礼佛，往行宫院休憩。

One kilometer to the west along the Changhe River from the Zhenjue Temple is the Wanshou Temple. It was built by Empress Dowager Li, mother of Emperor Wan Li of the Ming Dynasty, in 1578. In 1751 and 1761, Emperor Qian Long had it repaired and expanded on his mother's birthday. Gardens and a temporary palace were added, making it a royal temple.

Along the central line from south to north there are the front gate, Heavenly King Hall, Daxiong Hall, Wanshou Tower, Dachan Hall, Dashi Hall and Amitayus Hall. The eastern line is the abot's compound. The temporary palace was on the western line with grand buildings. During the Qing Dynasty, when the emperor and his consorts went to the Summer Palace and West Mountains on the river they would change boat at the Guangyuan Sluice east of the temple, come to the temple to present incense sticks and take a rest at the temporary palace.

俯瞰万寿寺 A bird's-eye-view of the temple.

万寿寺山门　门前的长河傍着古寺流淌，历经 400 多个春秋，景色依旧。

The front gate of the Wanshou Temple The Changhe River has flowed in front of the temple for more than 400 years.

药师佛 供奉在大雄宝殿内，为三世佛之一。佛经说众生只要敬念他的名号，就可解脱生老病死的苦难，免死于非命。

Statue of Bhaisajyaguru Boddha
Bhaisajyaguru is one of the Trikala Buddhas. Buddhists believe that if one chants his name with respect he will be spared of the pain of death.

十八罗汉　万寿寺内的罗汉塑得小巧玲珑，神态却生动逼真。

18 Arhats The 18 arhats in the Wanshou Temple are small and exquisite.

慈禧梳妆楼 建于行宫院北部，是清代慈禧太后（公元 1835－1908 年）来寺时的休憩之处。慈禧太后是清同治皇帝（公元 1862－1874 年在位）之母、光绪皇帝（公元 1875－1908 年在位）的伯母，她专横骄狂，同治、光绪两朝曾独揽朝纲近半个世纪。

Dressing Tower of Empress Dowager Ci Xi It is located in the northern part of the temporary palace. Empress Dowager Ci Xi (1835-1908) was mother of Emperor Tong Zhi of the Qing Dynasty and aunt of Emperor Guang Xi. She ruled China behind the curtain with absolute power nearly half a century.

通 教 寺
THE TONGJIAO TEMPLE

座落于城东东直门内，是一座颇为知名的尼寺。

寺原为明代太监所建，清代改建成尼寺，名通教禅林。至本世纪四十年代初，寺中殿宇倾颓，佛像残破，1942 年由福建来京的尼僧开慧、胜雨任寺中住持，她们募化钱财，对寺庙加以修葺、扩建，改名通教寺。

经扩建后的通教寺，占地 2500 平方米，建有山门、大雄宝殿、伽蓝殿、祖师殿、斋堂、寮房等，寺中房舍严整、环境幽雅，是一处净洁、雅致的修行之地。

寺中尼僧最多时达 70 余人，以修持戒律为本，在北京诸尼寺中，通教寺一向以戒规严格而著称。

The Buddhist temple in the eastern part of Beijing was built by eunuchs of the Ming Dynasty. It became a nunnery during the Qing Dynasty and was named Tongjiao. By the early 1940s the temple had been reduced to rambles. In 1942 Buddhist nuns Kai Hui and Sheng Yuren from Fujian Province came to become abots of the temple. They collected donations and restored the temple.

The expanded temple covered an area of 2,500 square meters. Main structures included the front gate, Daxiong Hall, Sangharama Hall, Masters' Hall, Fast Hall and living quarters. In its heyday, the temple had more than 70 nuns. The Tongjiao Temple was known for its strict discipline.

地藏菩萨像 供奉于大雄宝殿次间，佛经中说，地藏菩萨在释迦牟尼佛圆寂之后，弥勒佛未生之前，教化众生，拯救一切罪苦。

Statue of Ksitigarbha Buddha According to Buddhast scriptures, Ksitigarbha (Guardian of the Earth) is to deliver the suffering beings from the torments of the Hell after the death of Sakyamuni and before the birth of Maitreya (Future Buddha).

大雄宝殿内景 殿中供奉的主佛为阿弥陀佛。

Inside the Daxiong Hall The main Buddha worshipped in this hall is Amitabha.

大雄宝殿外景 大殿面积约 300 平方米，彩绘梁枋，绿琉璃瓦覆顶。

Outside the Daxiong Hall The 300-square-meter hall has brightly painted rafters and pillars and a green glazed tile roof.

永安寺
THE YONG'AN TEMPLE

建于北海公园琼华岛南坡。琼华岛是北海中的一座圆形山岛，从十一世纪起这里就成为皇家苑园，岛上遍布殿阁亭台，宛若仙境。公元1651年清代在前代废殿的基址上建起了一座藏式白色喇嘛塔，并在塔前建寺，从此，琼岛又名白塔山，寺亦名白塔寺。公元1743年重修后，更名永安寺。

白塔立于琼岛的中心，坐北面南，为永安寺的最高点。塔以南依次有善因殿、普安殿、正觉殿、法轮殿、山门、牌坊，从山顶延伸至山下，岛与岸之间有永安桥相连。

永安寺地处宫苑之内，美轮美奂，富有皇家气派。所有殿顶以黄绿两色琉璃瓦覆盖，殿脊上雕龙形图案；寺中山石亭台的配置，亦如皇宫御苑，与园内别处景致浑然一体。

The Yong'an Temple is located on the top of Qionghua Isle, a small circular man-made island in Beihai Lake in the center of Beijing. In the 11th century Beihai Lake was made an imperial garden. Towers and pavilions were built on the island. In 1651 the Qing court built a white pagoda of Tibetan style on the site of collapsed halls. The island was thus called White Pagoda Hill and the temple that housed the pagoda White Pagoda Temple. It was renamed Yong'an Temple when it was renovated in 1743.

The White Pagoda faces south and to its south there are the Shanyin Hall, Pu'an Hall, Zhengjue Hall, Hall of the Wheel of the Law, the front gate and an archway running from the top of the hill to the bank of Beihai Lake. The island is connected with the shore by the Yong'an Bridge.

The halls, though not as grand as halls in other Buddhist temples because of the limited space of the island, are beautifully decorated to display the imperial majesty. All the roofs are of yellow or green glazed tiles and have dragon carvings, a symbol of imperial palaces. The towers, pavilions and rockeries are also arranged according to imperial gardens.

永安寺全景 此寺殿堂自山脚步步递高，直至山顶白塔，布局独具特色。

The Yong'an Temple Its halls run up from the foot of the hill to the very top.

白塔 高踞于琼岛之巅，直插云天。塔高 35.9 米，塔内有高 28.8 米的通天柱，柱顶置金盒，内装舍利子。

White Pagoda Inside the 35.9-meter-high pagoda there is a 28.8-meter-high pillar. A gold box on top of the pillar contains Buddhist relics.

善因殿 位于白塔前，为仿木琉璃结构，上圆下方，顶为铜质筒瓦，镏金宝顶。方形殿内供千手千眼佛，殿外四周墙壁镶嵌着 445 尊琉璃佛像。

The Shanyin Hall The hall in front of the White Pagoda is built with glazed tiles in imitation of wood and has a roof of copper semi-circular tiles and a guilt crown. It is round on top and square below. Inside the hall there is a statue of Thousand-Hands-Thousand-Eyes Buddha. On the walls outside there are 445 Buddhist statues of glazed tiles.

普安殿脊的二龙戏珠琉璃雕饰

Two dragons playing with a pearl an ornament on the roof of the Pu'an Hall are made of glazed tiles.

雍 和 宫
THE YONGHEGONG LAMASERY

公元 1694 年清帝康熙在京城东北的安定门内为皇四子胤禛修建了一座富丽堂皇的府邸，二十八年后，这位皇子承继帝位，年号雍正（公元 1723—1735 年在位）。新帝迁入紫禁城，闲置的王府一半辟作藏传佛教格鲁派高僧修行的僧院，一半留作行宫。不久行宫被焚，剩余的一半于 1725 年改名为雍和宫，1744 年正式成为喇嘛寺。

由于雍和宫的前身为王府，所以它的建筑格局异于其它的寺庙，而宛若一座简缩了的王宫。宫门面南，由南至北在长约 480 米的中轴线上，排列着牌楼、昭泰门、天王殿、雍和宫大殿、永佑殿、法轮殿、万福阁、绥成楼等殿堂楼阁。宫东西宽近 120 米，在主要建筑的两翼，两两对称地建有钟鼓楼、碑亭、密宗殿和讲经殿、数学殿和药师殿、班禅楼和戒台楼、照佛楼和雅木达嘎楼、永康阁和延绥阁，以及东、西顺山楼，东、西配殿。

In 1694 Emperor Kang Xi built a grand mansion for his fourth son Yin Zhen inside the Anding city gate in the northeastern part of Beijing. Yin Zhen ascended the throne 28 years later and became known as Emperor Yong Zheng (reigned between 1723 and 1735). After he moved to the imperial palace half of his former residence became a temple for Yellow sect monks and half became a temporary palace. Soon after the temporary palace was burnt down. The temple was renamed Yonghegong in 1725. In 1744 it was formally announced a lamasary.

Because it was originally a residence of a prince, the temple is actually a samller imperial palace. Aong the central axile of 480 meters from south to north there are an archway, the Shaotai Gate, Heavenly King Hall, Yonghegong Main Hall, Yongyou Hall, Hall of the Wheel of the Law, Wanfu Tower and Suicheng Tower. The temple is 120 meters from east to west. Flanking the main structures along the central axile and arranged symestrically on either side there are the bell and drum towers, stele pavilion, Mizong Hall, Lecture Hall, Mathematics Hall, Bhaisajyaguru Hall, Panchen Tower, Ordination Tower, Zhaofu Tower, Yamudaka Tower, Yongkang Tower, Yansui Tower, Eastern and Western Shunshan Towers and wing halls.

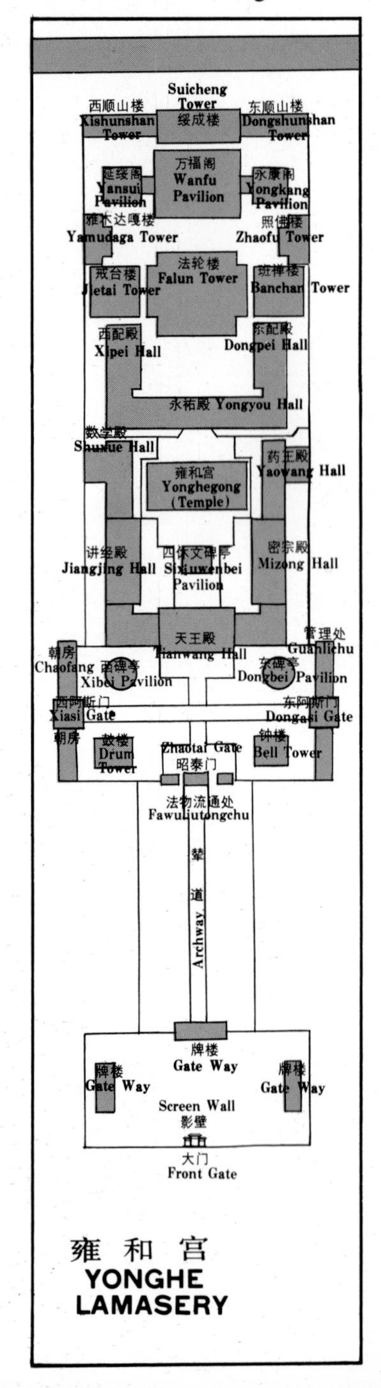

俯瞰雍和宫 但见殿阁重重，主次分明，排列有序。

A bird's-eye-view of the Yonghegong Lamasary.

宫中最大的铜鼎炉 铸于公元1747年，炉体呈青色，光可鉴人，纹饰精美，可与紫禁城御花园中的鼎炉媲美。

The largest bronze burner The largest bronze burner in the lamasery was cast in 1747. The well polished wall is like a mirror and bears elaborately carved designs. Its craftsmanship is as good as that of bronze burners in the Imperial Garden in the Forbidden City.

雍和宫殿 原是雍亲王府正殿银安殿，现等同一般寺院中的大雄宝殿，内供三世佛和十八罗汉。

Yonghegong Hall Originally it was the Yinan Hall of the Prince Yong Palace. After the palace became a lamasery the hall took the place of Daxiong Hall of other Buddhist temple. Inside the hall there are statues of Trikala Buddhas and 18 arhats.

法轮殿 融汉藏建筑风格于一体，是喇嘛诵经的经堂。

The Hall of the Wheel of the Law
The hall is a combination of Tibetan and central China architectural styles. It is where lamas chant prayers.

镏金宝塔　设置于法轮殿殿顶，仿藏传佛殿顶饰而建，共有五座，此为其一。

Guilt Pagoda　It is placed on top of the Hall of the Wheel of the Law built in Tibetan style. There are altogether five of guilt pagodas.

喇嘛在法轮殿诵经的情景 殿中央的坐像为藏传佛教格鲁派创立者宗喀巴大师。像高 6.1 米，铜质，是寺中喇嘛于本世纪二十年代筹资铸造的。

Lamas chanting prayer The copper 6.11-meter-high statue in the center of the Hall of the Wheel of the Law is of Tsongkhapa, founder the the Buddhist Yellow Sect. It was made in the 1920s with donations.

五百罗汉山 立于法轮殿，山体用紫檀木精雕而成，面积仅十数平方米，厚 30 厘米；山间布有五百尊高仅 10 厘米、用金银铜铁锡制成的罗汉，构成了一幅富有故事情节、意境颇浓的立体画，穷极工巧，故被称为雍和宫一绝。

500-Arhat Hall The sculpture of purple sandalwood in the Hall of the Wheel of the Law is 30 centimeters thick and a dozen square meters in area. The 500 arhats of 10 centimeters high are made of gold, silver, copper and tin depicting various stories. The sculpture of very high value for the craftsmanship.

万福阁　重檐三层、高达 25 米，居北京寺殿之冠，公元 1750 年专为供置弥勒佛巨像而建。

The Wanfu Tower　The 30-meter-high tower of three eaves is the highest in Beijing of its kind. It was built specially to house a giant Buddhist statue in 1750.

迈达拉佛（弥勒佛） 矗立于万福阁，像高 18 米，宽 8 米，全身贴金，镶嵌珠宝无数。像用高 26 米，直径 3 米余的白檀木雕成，这株奇木是七世达赖喇嘛以重金从尼泊尔访求得来，献给乾隆皇帝的。

Wandala Buddha The guilt statue in the Wanfu Tower is 18 meters high, eight meters wide. It was carved out a a whole piece of white sandalwood of 26 meters high and three meters in diameter. The wood was bought by the seventh Dalai Lama from Nepal and present it to Emperor Qian Long of the Qing Dynasty.

飞廊　分别搭造于万福阁和永康阁、延绥阁之间，使它们浑然一体，相连相通，外观犹如仙宫楼阙。

Flying Corridors　The corridors were built to connect the Wanfu, Yongkang and Yansui towers.

西 黄 寺
THE WEST HUANG TEMPLE

是藏传佛教格鲁派寺庙，位于城区北部安定门外。

寺建于公元1652年，因格鲁派僧人着黄色僧袍、戴黄帽，所以该派又称黄教，黄寺因之得名。此寺以东，原有一座建于公元1651年的藏传佛教寺院，为了便于区分，人们便依两寺方位称为东、西黄寺。东黄寺早已无存。

公元1780年，六世班禅大师巴丹益喜（公元1738－1780年）自西藏来京为乾隆皇帝祝寿，在京期间，曾驻锡寺中。同年，班禅大师在京逝世，乾隆皇帝令在寺北建衣冠石塔，名为"清净化城塔"。石塔为印度迦耶精舍形制，但又融进了藏、汉的建筑风格，至今保存完好，成为寺内最具有特色的建筑。

中国藏语系高级佛学院设于寺内，常年皆有藏、蒙族高僧在院内深造。

The Buddhist temple of the Yellow sect is located outside the Anding city gate north of the Beijing proper. Because monks of the Yellow sect wear yellow garments and hats, the temple is thus called Huang, or Yellow. There used to be another temple of the Yellow sect to tis east built in 1651 so the local people differentiated them by calling them the East and West Huang Temples. The East Huang Temple had long disappeared.

In 1780 Sixth Panchen Lama Badanyixi (1738-1780) came to Beijing for the birthday celebratio of Emperor Qian Long and satyed in the West Huang Temple. He died in the same year in Beijing. Emperor Qian Long ordered to built a stone stupa to keep the lama's clothes and hat. The stupa in the style of Indian Gaya temples is a combination of Indian, Tibetan and central China architecture.

The temple houses the China Academy of Buddhism teaching in Titetan language.

黄寺山门　为面阔三间的庑殿式建筑，顶覆黄绿两色琉璃筒瓦，在寺庙山门中，它是较有特色的一座汉式建筑。

Front gate　The gate in the imperial palace style has a roof of glazed tiles of yellow and green colors. It is outstanding for its central China architectural style.

俯瞰黄寺全景

A bird's-eye-view of the West Huang Temple.

清净化城塔夜景 五塔建于高 3.4 米的平台上，塔高 20 米。主塔正面佛龛内有三世佛浮雕像，龛旁分雕八尊菩萨像。

Night at the Jinghuacheng Stupas
The five stupas stand on a 3.4-meter-high terrace and are 20 meters high themselves. A relief in a niche on the front side of the main stupa depicts Trikla Buddhas. Flanking the niche there are eight statues of Bodhisattva.

主塔须弥座 座为八角形，每面都刻有以佛教故事为题材的精美浮雕。

The Sumeru Base of the main stupa
On the sides of the octagonal base are exquisite relief carvings depicting Buddhist stories.

觉 生 寺
THE JUESHENG TEMPLE

觉生寺，俗名大钟寺，在今北三环西路北侧。公元 1733 年寺初建时，此地尚是一处远离市嚣的寂静清修之地，如今寺的周围楼群林立，门前车水马龙，已处于延扩的新市区之内了。

寺的布局严谨对称，自南而北有影壁（已毁）、山门、天王殿、大雄宝殿、观音殿、藏经楼、大钟楼，方丈院位于寺的东侧。

寺初建成时并无出众之处，自公元 1743 年永乐大钟由万寿寺移入寺内，寺名遂随钟声播扬京城内外。

永乐大钟铸于明永乐年间（公元 1403–1424 年），它不仅体大量重，音质纯正，铸造精良，而且钟壁内外铸汉文、梵文经咒、铭文 100 余种，计 23 万余字，故有“钟王”之誉。1992 年评定的“北京十大旅游世界之最”，永乐大钟即居其一，被称为“世界上铭文字数最多的大钟”。

1985 年，在寺内辟建“大钟寺古钟博物馆”，专门收藏、研究、鉴定、展览中外各类钟、铃文物。

The Juesheng Temple is popularly known as the Giant Bell Temple because it houses a large bronze bell. It is located on the western part of the Third Circular Road north of the city proper. When the temple was built in 1733 the place was desolate. Now high-rise buildings and heavy traffic have long made the surroundings of the once quite Buddhist sanctuary a part of the busy city.

The layout of the temple is strictly symestrical. From south to north there are a screen wall, the front gate, Heavenly King Hall, Daxiong Hall, Avalokitesvara Hall, Scripture Tower and Giant Bell Tower. The abot living quarter is in a courtyard on the eastern side of the temple.

The temple became famous when in 1743 a giant bell casted in 1743 during the reign of Yong Le was moved into it from the Wanshou Temple. The bell was casted during the Yong Le period (1403-1424). It is of excellent craftsmanship and gives off beautiful sound which reaches to a very long distance. The inside and outside of the bell bear 230,000 words of Buddhist scriptures, incantations and notes in the Chinese and Sanskrit languages. In 1992 it was named as one of the ten World Records in Beijing for tourists. It has the largest number of words of inscriptions on it in the world.

In 1985 the Giant Bell Temple Ancient Bells Museum was established which collects, carries out research on and displays various bells and related relics.

大钟寺山门 门前有广场，每年农历正月初一至十五为大钟寺庙会期，届时广场上摊档相联，寺内外游人如织。

The front gate A temple fair is held between the first day to the 15th day of the first lunar month every year in the open ground in front of the gate. The fair attracts crowds of vendors and visitors.

大钟寺全景 The Giant Bell Temple.

大钟楼　为上圆下方的重檐建筑，既是悬挂大钟的需要，又寓有“天圆地方”之意。楼内设木梯，登梯上楼，可俯视大钟顶部。

The Yong Le Giant Bell　It is 6.75 meters high and 3.3 meters in diameter and weighs 46.5 tons. Its sound reaches as far as severla dozen kilometers.

永乐大钟 钟高 6.94 米，最大直径 4 米，重 46.5 吨，击之声闻十数公里，是名副其实的古钟之王。

Giant Bell of Yongle The "King of Bells" is 6. 94 meters high and 4 meters in diameter and weighs 46. 5 tons. Its sound can be heard over several dozen kilometers.

古钟陈列室之一

An exhibition room in the Giant Bell Temple.

大钟经文局部

Detail of the scripture inscribed on the bell.

编　　辑　廖　频　望天星
翻　　译　刘宗仁
摄　　影　何炳富　高明义　王春树
姜景余　望天星　张肇基
黄韬朋　刘　臣　严钟义
王文波　谷维恒　李　佐
张伶绵　朱金科　韦显文
国　伟　罗广林　邹宝义
李燕平　李元明　张旭东
何　伟　李建勇
装帧设计　唐　宇

Editors: Liao Pin and Wang Tianxing
Translated by: Liu Zongren
Photos by: He Bingfu, Gao Mingyi, Wang Chunshu, Jiang Jingyu, Wang Tianxing, Zhang Zhaoji, Huang Daopeng, Liu Chen, Yan Zhongyi, Wang Wenbo, Gu Weiheng, Li Zuo, Zhang Lingmian, Zhu Jinke, Wei Xianwen, Guo Wei, Luo Guanglin, Zhou Baoyi, Li Yanping, Li Yuanming, Zhang Xudong, He Wei and Li Jianyong
Designed by: Tang Yu

北京古刹名寺
廖 频 望天星编
刘宗仁 译核
*
中国世界语出版社出版
北京 1201 厂印制
中国国际图书贸易总公司发行
(中国北京车公庄西路 35 号)
北京邮政信箱第 399 号 邮政编码: 100044
1995年(16开)第一版第二次印刷
ISBN 7-5052-0118-2/K·21(外)
06800
85-CE-419 P